Accelerating K–8 Math Instruction

Resend ALN
- math guiding doc
- vision -
- commitments
- Star model
- Reading Catalyzing
  Change

Accelerating
K–8 Math
Instruction

A Comprehensive Guide to Helping All Learners

Dr. Nicki Newton

Foreword by Melanie Harding

TEACHERS COLLEGE PRESS

TEACHERS COLLEGE | COLUMBIA UNIVERSITY

NEW YORK AND LONDON

Visit www.tcpress.com/NewtonMath for downloadable content and templates.

Published by Teachers College Press®, 1234 Amsterdam Avenue, New York, NY 10027

Copyright © 2023 by Teachers College, Columbia University

Front cover design by Holly Grundon / BHG Graphics. Photos (clockwise from top left) by: Sasirin Pamai; FatCamera; SDI Productions; and coscaron, all via iStock by Getty Images.

Figures 1.1, 1.2, 1.4, 2.1, 2.2, 2.3, 2.4, 2.5, 2.6, 3.2, 3.3, 3.4, 4.1, 4.2, 4.3, 4.4A, 4.4B, 4.5, 4.6, 4.7, 5.2, 5.8A, 5.8B, 5.9, 5.12, 6.1, 6.2, 6.3, 6.4, 6.5, 6.8, 6.14, 6.15, 6.16, 6.17, 6.18, 6.19, 6.20, 6.21, 6.24, 6.25, 6.26, 6.27, 7.1, 7.2, 7.4, 7.5, 7.7A, 7.8D, 7.8E, 7.9, 7.13, 7.14, 7.15, 7.16, 7.19, 7.20, 7.21, 7.22, 7.23, 7.24A, 7.24B, 7.24C, 7.24D, 8.1, 8.2, 8.3, 8.4, 8.9, 8.18, 8.19, 8.20, 8.21, 8.22, 8.24, 8.28, 8.29, 8.30, 9.1, 9.2, 9.3, 9.4, 9.5, 9.6, and 9.8 © 2023 by Nicki Newton. Reprinted by permission of the author.

Library of Congress Cataloging-in-Publication Data is available at loc.gov

ISBN 978-0-8077-6816-7 (paper)
ISBN 978-0-8077-6817-4 (hardcover)
ISBN 978-0-8077-8163-0 (ebook)

Printed on acid-free paper
Manufactured in the United States of America

To Mom and Pops always

Contents

Foreword

As educators, we often talk about how to meet students' social and emotional needs. When we talk about social and emotional learning (SEL), we don't always think about mathematics instruction, but we need to. As a math educator, I think of our students who have gaps in learning due to the unprecedented disruption in education created by the COVID-19 pandemic and how it will affect their confidence when learning grade-level content. We know that the learning loss due to the pandemic was significant, on average leaving students five months behind in mathematics, and even more so for students in low-income schools.

Historically, when students experience any type of learning loss, educators swiftly administer a diagnostic assessment and place them into remediation groups for unintentional instruction in content below their grade level. This just-in-case learning only exacerbates equity issues, giving students a feeling of failure through deficit-based labels. Conversely, acceleration can positively impact students' motivation, self-efficacy, engagement, confidence, and participation. To build students' confidence and pride in their learning, it is imperative that teachers present grade-level content to *all*, while providing individualized, just-in-time scaffolds that students may need to learn grade-level math alongside their peers.

Recent studies have shown the extent to which lost instructional time is affecting student performance in both math and reading. The U.S. Department of Education (2021) reported that most students had made some learning gains in both reading and math since spring 2020; however, gains in math were lower than average compared to prior years. Another study similarly found that the achievement gaps in math that existed prior to the pandemic persisted over the past year, and in some cases widened (Dorn et al., 2020).

Dr. Nicki Newton's book, *Accelerating K–8 Math Instruction: A Comprehensive Guide to Helping Learners*, is the "just-in-time" tool that educators need at this unprecedented moment. Dr. Nicki's book is based on an extensive body of research in unfinished learning and the use of acceleration to recover the ground lost due to the pandemic. However, she goes a step further, asserting that this instructional model, which encompasses formative assessment, a deep understanding of standards, planning, progress monitoring, and goal setting, is a long-term framework that extends beyond the learning losses due to the pandemic. Her ideas about how to address learning loss and unfinished learning are grounded in research and best practices, and they should be a part of the work informed teachers do every day.

Working with teachers for many years as a mathematics coach and supervisor, I have used Dr. Nicki's expansive library of resources to enhance educators' practices in mathematics, with a focus on areas such as assessment, guided math, math workstations, fluency, running records, discourse, disposition, and so much more. This book is a welcome addition to that library of resources, and will be for years to come. Dr. Nicki offers hands-on, ready-to-implement approaches, frameworks, formats, schemas, planning and assessment tools, examples, engaging activities, and vocabulary building strategies, and her work exemplifies the ways that teachers can immediately begin accelerating instruction by intentionally tapping into prior knowledge. In addition to addressing the problem of skill gaps in the context of new learning, she tackles underlying causes of math deficiencies, such as student motivation and perseverance, as well as ways to build self-efficacy. Unlike any other resource teachers will use, this book is a valuable solution that provides educators with the tools they need to help *all* children reach their academic potential. Dr. Nicki's research-based practical methods for acceleration strategically address unfinished learning and prepare students for success while engaging the whole child in grade-level content. Students who come to school with learning gaps and attitudes about math can be greatly helped through acceleration and the effort teachers put toward this type of instruction. Let's face it, our children deserve it.

Melanie Harding
Mathematics Supervisor
Long Branch Public Schools, New Jersey

Dorn, E., Hancock, B., Sarakatsannis, J., & Viruleg, E. (2020). *COVID-19 and learning loss—Disparities grow and students need help.* McKinsey & Company. https://www.mckinsey.com/industries/public-and-social-sector/our-insights/covid-19-and-learning-loss-disparities-grow-and-students-need-help

U.S. Department of Education. (2021). *ED COVID-19 handbook: Vol. 2. Roadmap to reopening safely and meeting all students' needs.* OPEPD-IO-21-02. https://www2.ed.gov/documents/coronavirus/reopening-2.pdf

Acknowledgments

I thank God for life and an opportunity to write more. I am grateful to my mom and dad for all the opportunities they set me up for and to my grandparents for their dreams and hopes for future generations. I thank all my family and friends for their continued support along the journey. To all the teachers and students I work with who teach me new things every day, thank you. I am grateful to Jean Ward for encouraging me to write this book and to Allison Scott for helping to see it through. I thank Melanie Harding for being gracious enough to write a wonderful foreword and Christine Mulgrave King for contributing her beautiful story as the epilogue. I appreciate the work of the entire team that helped put this together: the copyeditors, the art editors, the production team, and everybody who had a hand in making it happen. I value the work of Lynne Frost, who is one of the best copyeditors in the business. Finally, I thank the future readers for taking time out of your busy schedules to share in my thinking. May this book help you along your journey of making the world a better place to teach and learn.

Introduction

A lot has happened in education as a result of the COVID-19 pandemic. The realities are front and center now that our students have come back to school in person, though some have subsequently returned to online learning again. Some students learned a great deal while they were out of the classroom. Some flourished doing online learning. All learned to persevere, to become more competent with technology, and to expand their skill sets of learning how to learn.

However, many learners struggled academically. We know from the research that many students wrestled with social and emotional needs and academic learning loss (U.S. Department of Education, 2021)—or what others have termed "unfinished learning." Many argue that labeling these setbacks "learning loss" reflects a deficit perspective and situates the problem with the students. Others contend that students could not have lost something they possibly never had learned. And still others point out that they didn't have the same opportunity to learn everything online that they would have had in the classroom. Referring to this phenomenon as "unfinished learning" highlights the fact that the students did not learn the same things in the same ways they would have, had they been in school in person (Dorn et al., 2021). This framing also implies that students can and will continue to learn with excellent instruction.

The idea of "learning loss" is not new. Anderson (2020) wrote an essay discussing "summer learning loss" and comparing what happens with literacy and with math. That article looks at how students lose much more math over the summer months than they do literacy and considers ways to address these losses. Other research on learning loss has addressed how it occurs during seasonal breaks, interruptions in education, absences from school, and periods of inadequate teaching (Atteberry, 2016; Nisbet, 2021; Cooper et al., 1996). Nisbet notes that "the educational term *'learning loss'* refers to the reversal of academic performance or loss of knowledge and skills, often as a result of external factors such as planned and unplanned school closures." Given this definition, undoubtedly there was some learning loss during the pandemic, but all the preexisting challenges students faced were exacerbated during this time, and setbacks cannot be attributed only to learning loss.

The term *unfinished learning* refers to "concepts or skills in which students were in the process of learning but unable to master, or never had the opportunity to learn" (Nisbet, 2021). This term more fully describes what happened during the pandemic. The difficulties that students are having today with mathematics learning can drastically impact their overall learning trajectory in the future. Incoming data for the 2020–2021 school year show a continuing crisis in education worldwide that has been worsened by the pandemic (World Bank, 2021). Students learned what they could online, some more than others, but they did not grasp it in the way they would have in person or even to the depths of understanding that they actually needed to.

Referring to something as "unfinished" implies that it can be finished. It implies that there is hope. It implies that the learning struggles can be addressed. There is not nearly enough research on unfinished learning, but the body of knowledge is growing. The Thomas B. Fordham Institute (2021) notes that research evidence shows that students are returning to school with "a substantial amount of unfinished learning." Schools are wanting to test students and group them and set them to work on a bunch of "below-grade-level work," which the Institute recommends is not the approach that should be taken. They argue that there is an emerging consensus that acceleration—teaching students on grade level with needed supports—is the way to go, along with high-dosage tutoring.

Researchers initially found that although things improved somewhat during the 2020–2021 school year, with most students getting back to in-person learning, the impact of the pandemic left students "on average five months behind in mathematics and four months behind in reading by the end of the school year" (Dorn et al., 2021). Educators today are scrambling to fill knowledge and skill gaps that first occurred for some students, and grew for others, during the pandemic and are showing up in different ways as we return to in-person schooling.

To make matters worse, "many student groups [who struggled in unproductive ways with academic learning] in school prior to the pandemic—primarily students from low socioeconomic communities and Black, Latinx, and Indigenous students—were disproportionately impacted during the pandemic, resulting in further widening of achievement gaps" (Fong, 2021), or what many have more aptly termed the "opportunity gap" (Milner, 2012). We have to do something to address the students who are unproductively struggling with mathematics. This work has been termed *learning recovery*.

Much recent research recommends we focus on tackling learning recovery with acceleration rather than remediation. The U.S. Department of Education (2021) suggests that schools focus on strategies that accelerate learning. Four evidence-based strategies (which can be used individually or in combination) to catch students up academically are offered (see Figure I.1):

1. In-school acceleration
2. High-quality tutoring

Figure I.1. Four Recommendations for Addressing Students Struggling With Math

In-School Acceleration	• Can be done by the core teacher or a supplemental teacher • Usually at least 30-minute sessions • At least 3× a week
High-Quality Tutoring	• Can be done by the core teacher or a supplemental teacher • Usually at least 30-minute sessions • At least 3× a week
Before, After, or Weekend School	• Teachers can meet with an acceleration group • Tutors can meet for 1:1 or small-group sessions
Summer Learning and Enrichment	• School hosts a summer program • Program focuses on intervention and enrichment • Usually at least 30-minute sessions • At least 3× a week

3. Programs offered outside of school hours
4. Summer learning and enrichment

The U.S. Department of Education (2021) suggests that schools should spend the time, energy, funds, and effort on strategies that *accelerate* student learning. When developing their local acceleration plan, schools must consider their students' academic needs, available resources, and partnerships with local and national organizations that may be able to assist.

Fong (2021) has found that "accelerated learning ensures that students, especially those who have experienced the greatest learning losses, are consistently instructed with grade-level materials, are provided scaffolding and are gaining the most critical just-in-time content knowledge and skills needed to access curricula at the appropriate grade level." Really, the work is about "ensuring equity, excellence and achievement for all students, regardless of background" (Ken Williams, personal communication).

ACCELERATION IS NOT REMEDIATION

It is very important to recognize that acceleration is different from remediation. Remediation is focused on filling in all the gaps remaining from prior grades and putting off the current grade-level content. Rollins (2014) notes that "instead of addressing gaps in the context of new learning and helping students succeed in class today, remedial programs largely engage students in activities that connect to standards from years ago. Rather than build students' academic futures, remediation pounds away at the past. We spend significant amounts of time teaching in reverse, and then ask why students are not catching up to their peers."

This book has been written to help educators unpack accelerating instruction. It endeavors to show us how acceleration provides a pathway to helping academically challenged students achieve and move in step with their grade-level standards. It is about understanding how we use effective, research-based strategies that move students forward rather than keep them mired in the work of past grades. This book is full of tools, templates, and blackline masters that will help you consider, unpack, brainstorm, and plan for acceleration in elementary and middle school classrooms.

"Neither retention nor social promotion constitutes a viable academic plan for struggling students."   —Rollins (2014)

Historically, we have addressed students who are struggling with math in one of three ways (see Figure I.2). The first thing we have done is retain them and make them repeat the grade. Research shows that many students who have been retained eventually drop out. We have so much research against retention, but we still do it (David, 2008; Kamin & Lamb, 2021). The second thing we have done is socially promote them. Even though they are not ready for the upcoming grade, we send them happily along, unprepared, without scaffolds to support their journey (David, 2008; Frey, 2005). The third thing we have done is remediate all year long. We spend hours of time, effort, and energy on trekking through the shadows of past concepts and skills that have absolutely no connection to what students are currently learning.

TERMS WE NEED TO KNOW

Acceleration. Acceleration is teaching students on grade level with math intervention support. The intervention specifically reaches back to targeted and relevant prerequisite skills and concepts from the previous grade as necessary, scaffolding students as needed to grade-level learning.

Figure I.2. Traditional Approaches When Students Struggle With Math

Retention	Students who are not working on grade level are retained and required to repeat the grade.
Social Promotion	Students continue on with their age peers, regardless of their academic achievement.
Remediation	Students work in remedial groups, relearning and reviewing all the past standards, trying to fill in all the things they do not know or are struggling to do.

Learning Loss. By learning loss, I am referring to the idea that students have lost some of what they knew (ideas, concepts, skills, and strategies) before the pandemic. They have come back to school not knowing certain information or much weaker, having lost what they knew before they left. Learning loss has also been used to refer to the idea that students did not get the grade-level knowledge or skills that they would have acquired in a regular, in-person school year. Not all students experienced learning loss. Families who had "better access to resources, including financial resources, stable employment, flexible work from home and childcare arrangements" may have been able to negotiate the pandemic situation better than those families who experienced housing and food instability or other traumatic events due to the pandemic (i.e., health and welfare challenges) (Colorado Department of Education, n.d., p. 2).

Learning Loss Recovery. Learning loss recovery has been defined as "steps that research recommends schools and districts should take to recover learning loss that occurred due to extended and repeated school closures combined with remote learning. This definition applies to school-wide efforts for large groups of students. This definition does not include recovery of learning for individual[s] or small groups of students" (Colorado Department of Education, n.d., p. 1).

Priority Standards. The standards that students must know to mastery level for the designated grade. Each state has its own set of readiness/major, focus standards. This book focuses on standards that are generally accepted across most states.

Remediation. Remediation means to remedy, which is the "act of correcting a problem" (Merriam-Webster, n.d.). Many traditional math intervention programs are designed to go back and try to fix all the gaps, misconceptions, error patterns, and misunderstandings that students have had throughout their educational journey.

Scaffolding. Scaffolding is a process that involves helping students learn what they need to know by using a series of supports that are slowly faded out as students no longer need them. An acceleration cycle of learning includes various types of scaffolds that allow students to access grade-level learning on an as-needed basis. Teachers must be careful not to overscaffold or underscaffold. Scaffolding must be done "just in time," not "just in case," as Dixon (2020) points out.

Unfinished Learning. Some scholars have suggested that the term unfinished learning is a more appropriate way to describe what is often called "learning loss." "Unfinished learning" refers to the concepts that students have yet to master from previous grades. It is a term used to reframe words like "weakness" or "gap" to put an emphasis on the idea that these things will be learned, but just have not been learned yet. Many have argued that the term learning loss (see above) is insufficient as well as inaccurate to describe the situation. Others have argued that we should use the term unfinished instruction to better describe the "combination of teaching and learning within an academic [time that failed] to provide students with an opportunity to demonstrate proficiency with grade levels tests and tasks" (Hancock, 2021).

*   *   *

In this book, we are going to take a deep dive into in-school acceleration. In the chapters that follow, we will discuss the following:

- Research on acceleration
- Planning for acceleration
- Unpacking prior knowledge: Assessment as the key to acceleration
- Acceleration and the teaching of math vocabulary
- Acceleration lesson plan format
- Acceleration and pedagogy
- Acceleration in a primary math classroom
- Acceleration in an upper elementary math classroom
- Acceleration in a middle school classroom
- Goal setting and motivation

Readers of this book will find the perspectives, practices, and tools to help them scaffold students to grade level, enabling their students to learn grade-level math alongside their peers, which will give the students confidence and pride in learning math at grade level. Educators will in turn experience reduced frustration and the joy of helping students thrive.

Visit www.tcpress.com/NewtonMath for downloadable content and templates.

CHAPTER 1

Research on Acceleration

> Acceleration is the concept [and process] of teaching grade-level material but weaving in stopping points periodically to address a small missing piece in fundamental understanding before popping back up to the original skill. This concept is intended to overcome the vicious circle of reviewing below-grade-level concepts with struggling learners repeatedly, never giving them sufficient opportunity to demonstrate grade-level mastery.
>
> —Mitchell (2021)

WHAT IS ACCELERATION? WHAT IS THE SHIFT?

Acceleration is a paradigm shift. It moves away from schlepping students through the fields of everything they don't know and instead targets interventions that serve as a footbridge into the right now. Acceleration helps all students to be in the "know." It prepares them for upcoming lessons so that they can actively participate with their peers exploring grade-level standards. Acceleration is a way of saying, "Everybody is invited to this party." Acceleration is about teaching all students on grade level while specifically connecting back to targeted prior standards to scaffold success with the new ones. As Suzie Pepper Rollins (2014) explains, "Acceleration jump-starts under-performing students into learning new concepts before their classmates even begin. Rather than being stuck in the remedial slow lane, students move ahead of everyone into the fast lane of learning. Acceleration provides a fresh academic start for students every week and creates opportunities for struggling students to learn alongside their more successful peers" (p. 6). Figure 1.1 explains the elements of accelerated learning, and Figure 1.2 compares acceleration and remediation.

"Rather than build students' academic futures, remediation pounds away at the past. We spend significant amounts of time teaching in reverse, and then ask why students are not catching up to their peers."   —Rollins (2014)

Figure 1.1. Elements of Accelerated Learning

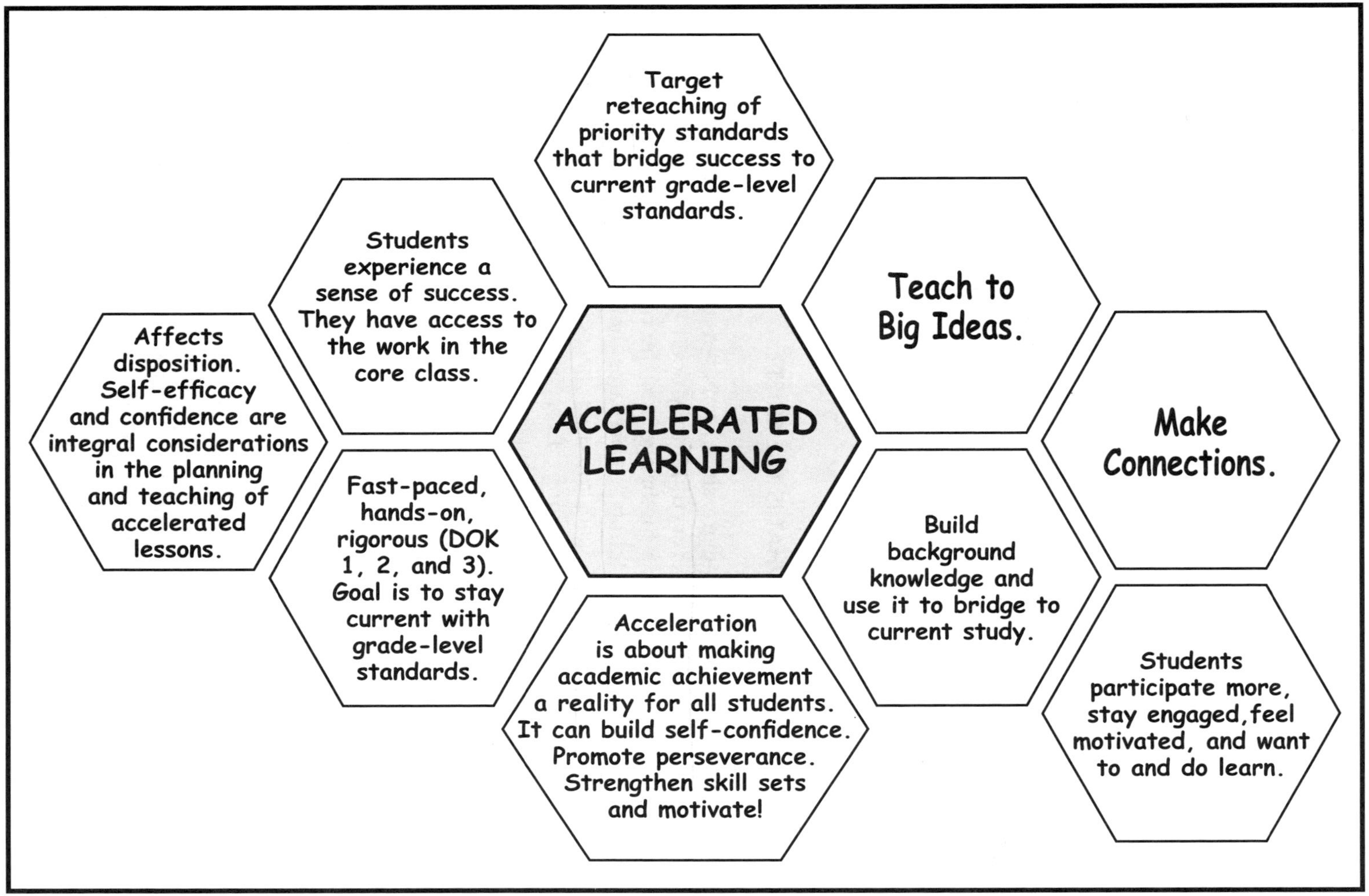

ACCELERATED LEARNING

Make Connections.

Students participate more, stay engaged, feel motivated, and want to and do learn.

Teach to Big Ideas.

Build background knowledge and use it to bridge to current study.

Target reteaching of priority standards that bridge success to current grade-level standards.

Acceleration is about making academic achievement a reality for all students. It can build self-confidence. Promote perseverance. Strengthen skill sets and motivate!

Students experience a sense of success. They have access to the work in the core class.

Fast-paced, hands-on, rigorous (DOK 1, 2, and 3). Goal is to stay current with grade-level standards.

Affects disposition. Self-efficacy and confidence are integral considerations in the planning and teaching of accelerated lessons.

Figure 1.2. Remediation Versus Acceleration

	Math Intervention	
	Remediation	**Acceleration**
Goal	• Review content and skills from prior grades • Not much emphasis on vocabulary • Rarely are connections made to real life • Curiosity isn't provoked • Math isn't made relevant • Working on prior skills from years back—no connection to present work • Fill in all the gaps • Fix everything • Often unconnected with current grade level	• Acceleration is about teaching all students on grade level while specifically connecting back to targeted prior standards to scaffold success with the new ones—the present, this week • Clearly defined success criteria (learning goals and expectations) • Rich grade-level experiences (usually ahead of being introduced in class) • Bridge back to prior standards • Introduce and work with vocabulary • Revisit basic skills that are needed for current grade-level content • Never teach skills in isolation • Strategic, targeted addressing of prior knowledge and skills
Focus	Reteach everything from prior years; close all gaps.	Target reteaching of priority standards for individuals, groups, or whole class that bridge success to current grade-level standards.
Lesson Types: • Concrete explorations • Pictorial explorations • Abstract explorations	• Unfortunately, many remedial lessons are drill-and-kill worksheets that only add to the boredom, frustration, and dismay of students.	• Students do the work and it is graded and given back. • Ongoing formative assessment: Progress monitoring Student reflection Teacher feedback
Pacing	Pacing slow; worksheets; computer games; reaching back to prior standards, vocabulary, and skills (Depth of Knowledge [DOK] Level 1) (Webb, 2002).	Fast-paced, hands-on, rigorous (DOK 1, 2, 3). Goal is to stay current with grade-level standards.

(Continued on the next page)

Figure 1.2. Remediation Versus Acceleration *(continued)*

Affect	• Affect, disposition, self-efficacy, and confidence not a big part of planning for lessons.	• Affect, disposition, self-efficacy, and confidence are integral considerations in the planning and teaching of accelerated lessons.
	• Often students feel like they are in the "slow class."	• Students experience a sense of success.
	• They take on a disposition of helplessness and not knowing; sometimes they give up trying.	• They have access to the work in the core class.
General Observations	• Remediation is reteaching everything students did not learn in the prior grades. It's holding students hostage to vocabulary, concepts, and skills from two to three or more prior grades.	• Acceleration is not just a quick pre-teaching lesson. Acceleration is an instructional approach to teach students on grade level who are struggling in mathematics.
	• Students are doing lessons that do not connect to the new lesson.	• The activities are unique to the lesson. They are not repeated in the core lesson.
		• Rollins (2014) refers to it as "the core" and "the more." The core content and the supplemental learning and support that are provided by acceleration.

WHY DO WE ACCELERATE?

Acceleration is an instructional strategy that allows us to help students who are struggling with unfinished learning, academic gaps, misunderstandings, and persistent error patterns. In the era of COVID-19, students who already may have had some big gaps find the problem compounded by initial periods of virtual schooling, ongoing openings and shutdowns, and a return to class to cope with content that they may have missed some of the prerequisites for. Acceleration allows us to address these difficulties in ways that motivate students, help them track and build their self-confidence, and help them stay engaged, persevere, and achieve success. Acceleration is about making academic achievement a reality for all students. It can build self-confidence, promote perseverance, strengthen skill sets, and motivate! Students participate more, stay engaged, feel motivated, and want to and do learn.

WHAT ARE THE BENEFITS OF ACCELERATING?

There are many benefits to accelerating instruction, as shown briefly in Figure 1.3. Since students are prepared for the content, they can access it. They

Figure 1.3. Benefits of Acceleration

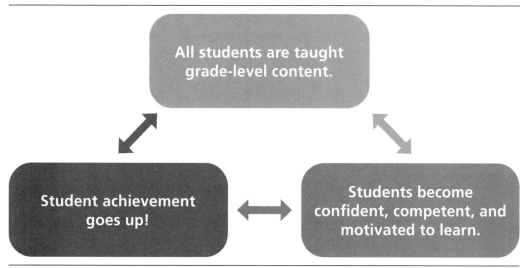

come to class ready to do the work, certain that they will be able to follow along. Acceleration helps students gain confidence in themselves as learners, the belief that they can do the work, and the competence to do the work. Acceleration also helps to address the social–emotional issues of frustration and disengagement that sometimes are exhibited by students who are angry with a system that does not seem to be serving them.

HOW DO WE ACCELERATE?

We accelerate by dropping back to the specific standard that provides the prior knowledge for the current standard. A trace of division from 6th grade through 3rd grade (see Figure 1.4) shows the progression and needed prior knowledge. At any one of these grades, if students are having trouble with the grade-level standard, the teacher can drop back and then scaffold up to the current big ideas, understandings, and skills.

SUMMARY

Schools have been using various approaches to address the struggles that students are having with math that have been compounded by the pandemic. There is an overwhelming consensus that we need to use acceleration rather than remediation. Acceleration is about equity. Acceleration allows all our students to access an engaging, standards-based, academically rigorous grade-level curriculum. We have to figure out how to do this well. We accelerate so that

- all students learn and work on grade level,
- all students get the exact "just right" scaffolding when they need it, and
- all students get to feel a sense of achievement and success.

Acceleration gets everybody motivated to learn and creates pathways of achievement. This is a paradigm shift, and we need to make sure that teachers have the knowledge base and pedagogy to do this really well. It can be done and should be done for the benefit of everyone!

Figure 1.4. A Division Trace

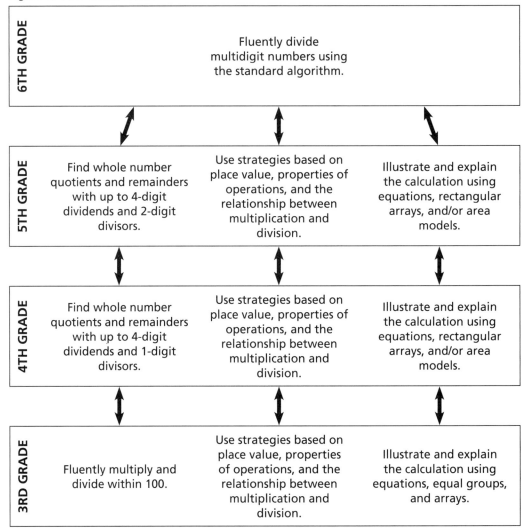

CHAPTER 2

Planning for Accelerated Lessons

The Importance of Prior Knowledge

> Acceleration is about making prior knowledge usable. It's really that simple. Acceleration is like using a jumper cable connected to a battery (prior knowledge) to start the engine of learning.

THE IMPORTANCE OF PRIOR KNOWLEDGE

Prior knowledge is all our memories, experiences, and understandings about a topic (The All-Access Classroom, n.d.). Prior knowledge scaffolds access to new knowledge. Hattie (2018) points out that prior knowledge has an effect size of 0.94, which is a very significant effect. Making use of prior knowledge is an important part of the learning process. It is extremely important in mathematics because math concepts build on each other. As students are learning new knowledge, their brains try to make connections between the old knowledge and the new. The brain wants to link and integrate the new knowledge with prior knowledge and experiences.

Brod et al. (2013) argued that prior knowledge helps us to learn faster because using it frees up students' working memory so they can digest new information more quickly. Marzano (2004) also points out that students who have prior knowledge on a topic can grasp new information on that topic quickly and well. Willis (2006) discusses how building connections between prior knowledge and new knowledge stimulates brain cell activity and leads to improved long-term memory and retrieval. Conversely, a lack of prior knowledge can vastly slow down the process and make learning new concepts very difficult (Rollins, 2014).

This is why acceleration works! Acceleration is based on the premise that we bridge new knowledge to prior knowledge directly, explicitly, and in a targeted way. We look at exactly the current concepts and skills we need students to learn and we tie them directly back to what came before that specific material. Nothing is wasted. Students learn on grade level. It all makes sense. Students are also given the scaffolds to use the prior knowledge content and skills needed to access the new information.

"Rather than concentrating on a litany of items that students have failed to master, acceleration readies students for new learning."   —Rollins (2014)

WHAT PRIOR KNOWLEDGE SHOULD BE PRIORITIZED?

Students in remediation class are schlepping through all the standards of the prior grade, with no particular focus and no connection to what they are currently learning. Remediation is framed in a belief system that says unless they know everything that came before they can't learn this new thing. Acceleration is framed in a belief system that all students can learn all things when those things are scaffolded, connected, and differentiated. "Acceleration strategically prepares all students for success in the present"—this week, this lesson, this unit (Rollins, 2014).

TRICKINESS OF PRIOR KNOWLEDGE

Teachers must find out what students know, think they know, and are totally confused about. Prior knowledge is complex. It has many facets. We have to know how to unpack it and work with it. Loft (2019) points out that prior knowledge can be any of the following:

- *Correct*—The learner has it and can use it (most of time)
- *Inactive*—The learner has it and can tap into it and use it
- *Insufficient*—The learner does not have it
- *Inappropriate*—The learner isn't making the right connections
- *Inaccurate*—The learner does not have it and is confused

We have to know the kinds of knowledge that students have. Ambrose et al. (2010) point out that "knowing *what* is a very different kind of knowledge than knowing *how* or knowing *when*." They argue that we should assess prior knowledge so we can know what to teach. We should activate prior knowledge so students can make the relevant connections. We are not only activating prior knowledge, we are building on prior knowledge. Ambrose et al. (2010) note that it is important to address misconceptions, and that they are sometimes very tricky to correct. Sometimes, it is easy to correct misinformation but at other times it is really difficult. It takes students several learning opportunities to "revise deeply held misconceptions. Instead, guiding students through a process of conceptual change is likely to take time, patience, and creativity" (p. 27).

Roberts (2018) points out that students said that the two things that frustrate them the most are these:

1. When I [student] *have* relevant prior knowledge and you [teacher] don't know it, or don't acknowledge it, I feel frustrated and annoyed.
2. When I [student] *do not have* relevant prior knowledge and you [teacher] carry on as though I do, I feel humiliated and embarrassed.

This is powerful. We must have ways to know what students know and what they have yet to learn. We have to know how to tap into their prior knowledge and use it.

It is important to assume nothing. You don't want to assume that students have knowledge they don't have and thus don't need to do a lesson. You don't want to assume that they don't have knowledge they might have. You must find out what they know and then determine how to use it. Gonzalez et al. (2005) write about the need to tap into our students' "funds of knowledge." There is formal knowledge and informal knowledge that we should be trying to learn about. All our students come with rich histories full of experiences that have led them to this moment. We must know how to tap into each and every one of those experiences.

THE ROLE OF PRIOR KNOWLEDGE IN ACCELERATING MATH

Prior knowledge is a bridge to success. Therefore, it is a crucial component of acceleration. We make direct connections between what we need to know and what we are currently learning. Rather than random, unfocused remediation on all topics in the world, the core and acceleration teachers work collaboratively and strategically to lay out a targeted pathway leading from the prior knowledge to the new concepts. To accelerate, we must know the vertical learning progressions across grades. These progressions allow us to trace prior standards along the learning pathway. Recently some great digital learning progressions have been created. One of the best is from Achieve (Achieve.org).

"They're already coming with so many experiences that we can tap into. These experiences help them to create connections to the content we want them to learn."

—Lundgren (n.d.)

EXPLICITLY TAPPING INTO PRIOR KNOWLEDGE

During an acceleration cycle, teachers need to intentionally and strategically tap into prior knowledge. It is also important to talk with the students about tapping into prior knowledge. There are many different activities that you can do with them to help them begin using their prior knowledge to make connections to the new knowledge. Tools such as prior knowledge talk cards, posters, mind maps, and more are illustrated in Figures 2.1–2.7. (All figures for this chapter are grouped at the end of the chapter.)

Posters for Activating Prior Knowledge

Posters such as the ones shown in Figures 2.3 and 2.4 can be used to support discussions with students about using their prior knowledge to connect to the new idea. Oftentimes teachers are only thinking about how they might take advantage of the prior knowledge/schema of the students. We rarely get students to talk actively about using their prior knowledge/schema in math class.

Metacognition Prompts

We can make anchor charts that help students think about their thinking and scaffold the language they might use to talk about their thinking. The metacognition prompts in Figure 2.5 can be used as a poster or as stems for students to get started journaling about what they are thinking in connection with new learning.

Graphic Organizers to Tap into Prior Knowledge

Graphic organizers help students organize their thinking. A blank mind map like that in Figure 2.6 is a great way to ask students to write down everything they know about the new topic, connecting items with arrows, bubbles, dotted and straight lines, or whatever helps them map their knowledge.

SCHEMA/PRIOR KNOWLEDGE MAPS

KWL charts (introduced by Ogle, 1986) are often useful in exploring a student's prior knowledge. Schema maps are another interesting option. Beth Ann (Adventures of a Schoolmarm, n.d.) uses schema maps in her classroom. She uses a wall chart that is "living": It changes as students add new information to it. She notes, "Schema maps require students to distinguish between information that is expanding upon something they already knew and information that is *brand new* learning" (see Figure 2.7). When creating schema maps with students, begin by having them write down on sticky notes everything they know, understand, and believe about a topic. Giving them sticky notes of various sizes can be helpful. Then the teacher puts up all the sticky notes on the map. If there is not agreement between some posts or if a thought is not certain, these comments can be put on a Post-it of a different color or flagged in some way to indicate that the students are still thinking about that point. Eventually, students will move the incorrect information to a spot on

Research Note: The correlation between academic background knowledge and achievement is staggering: Prior knowledge can determine whether a 50th-percentile student sinks to the 25th percentile or rises to the 75th.   —Marzano (2004)

the map that indicates it was not correct. When the students do this, they can then explain why that information was incorrect. As students learn new knowledge, they put that up on a sticky note of yet a different color.

Beth Ann points out that where you create the map is important: You need the space to see it. The sticky notes allow you to "visually distinguish prior knowledge, new knowledge and misconceptions." She uses three colors: one for prior knowledge, one for new learning, and one for things that are uncertain.

As they update their schema map, students are talking every day about what they knew and connecting it with what they are learning. And they are talking about what they had misunderstood originally. Beth Ann notes, "At the end of the unit you have this visual road map of the unit of study with markings of the journey along the way."

SUMMARY

Prior knowledge is an essential part of the acceleration process. We must develop ways to encourage students to actively tap into their prior knowledge and use it to make connections. We also have to identify prior knowledge that students will need so they can access the grade-level content. And we may have to build some of that knowledge because students just won't have it all.

Students do bring a lot of knowledge to the classroom. Maybe it is not all academic, but the informal knowledge can be part of what we must use to bridge into the new knowledge. For example, students may struggle with division, but they know how to divide real stuff in real life. The more we can tap into all the ways that students might know about something and make connections to it, the better we can teach the grade-level content.

Figures 2.1–2.7 appear on pages 18–24.

Figure 2.1. Prior Knowledge Tappers

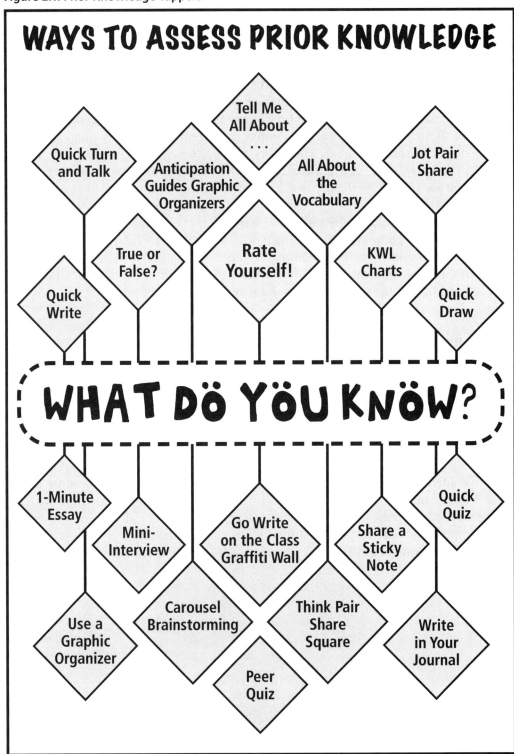

Figure 2.2. Prior Knowledge Cards

Students can shuffle through these cards and choose a new idea to talk about.

TAPPING INTO WHAT I KNOW

Have I heard of this before?

TAPPING INTO WHAT I KNOW

Where have I seen this in real life?

TAPPING INTO WHAT I KNOW

Is this easy or tricky for me?

TAPPING INTO WHAT I KNOW

What do I remember about learning about this in other grades?

TAPPING INTO WHAT I KNOW

Have I heard these words before?

TAPPING INTO WHAT I KNOW

Draw a sketch of what comes to mind when you hear this topic.

TAPPING INTO WHAT I KNOW

Use the Web to brainstorm everything you know about this topic.

Figure 2.3. Anchor Charts: Activating Prior Knowledge

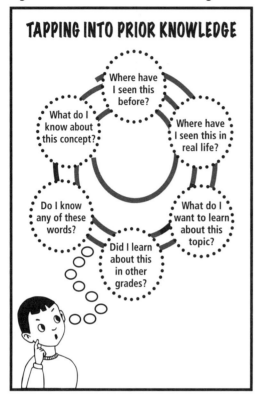

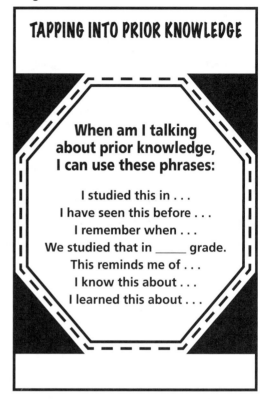

TAPPING INTO PRIOR KNOWLEDGE

When am I talking about prior knowledge, I can use these phrases:

I studied this in . . .
I have seen this before . . .
I remember when . . .
We studied that in _____ grade.
This reminds me of . . .
I know this about . . .
I learned this about . . .

Prior knowledge helps us connect old stuff to new stuff.
Those connections help us to learn faster
and learn more!

To make sense of the math they are learning,
good mathematicians . . .

- Think about what they know about the topic.
- Think about what they know about the vocabulary.
- Think about the models they have used.
- Think about how they have studied this in other grades.
- Think about how they have seen this in real life.

Prior knowledge is everything we already know about the
topic. We can use that to get our brains moving
and make connections to the new topic!

Figure 2.4. Prior Knowledge Poster

WHAT IS PRIOR KNOWLEDGE?

Our brain grows every time we learn new things!

We can make learning easier by connecting the old stuff to the new stuff!

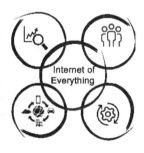

Prior knowledge is everything we have ever learned about this topic and everything we already know!

Good mathematicians ACTIVATE their prior knowledge to learn more!

Figure 2.5. Metacognition Prompts

METACÖGNITIÖN

We can think about our thinking . . .

 I'm thinking . . .

 I'm remembering . . .

 I'm noticing . . .

 I'm wondering . . .

 This reminds me when . . .

 I just realized . . .

Figure 2.6. Prior Knowledge Mind Map

PRIOR KNOWLEDGE MIND MAP

I am learning to use what I already know to help me learn new things.

Figure 2.7. Living Schema Map

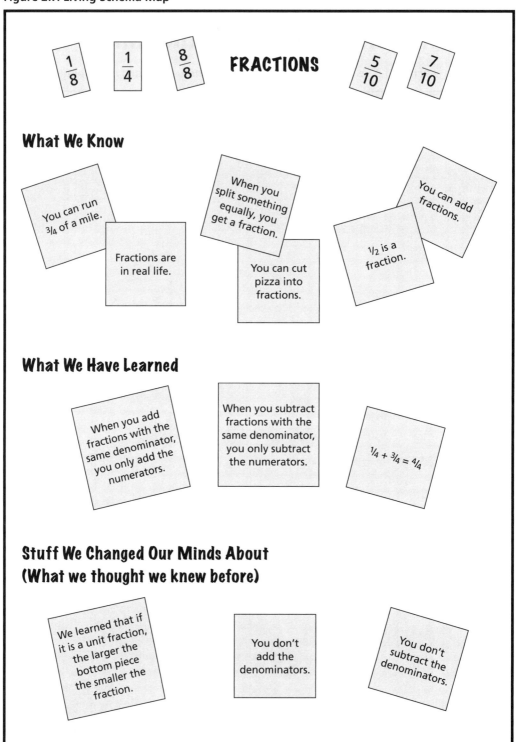

CHAPTER 3

Acceleration and the Teaching of Math Vocabulary

Active, strategic, targeted teaching of vocabulary is an important component of acceleration. Marzano (2004) points out that some of the students' gaps in disciplinary knowledge are related to vocabulary. Having gaps in vocabulary is a problem for many students learning math, and the problem is exacerbated for students who are struggling in math. Vocabulary poses problems for students in many ways—from standardized tests, class conversations, teacher lectures to word problems and more (Rollins, 2014). A poor academic vocabulary can be "academically debilitating" (Rollins, 2014). Acceleration familiarizes students with the words they will need so that when they encounter them in the core lesson, they will understand them. They feel empowered because they are ready for what is to come.

Research has found that direct, strategic, multisensory instruction in math vocabulary is very important for all students (Hiebert & Kamil, 2005; Kelly et al., 2010; Mancilla-Martinez, 2010; Scott et al., 2003). Word problems cause an extra layer of difficulty. Smith et al. (2012) found that in general there is a great deal of reading and comprehension involved with learning math. Marzano (2004) calculated the amount of essential math vocabulary that students are exposed to at different grade levels. He has a notable 30-word core vocabulary list for each grade. Every math program has its own suggested vocabulary for the unit of study, and many districts have key vocabulary words by grades.

Beck et al. (2013) theorized a three-tier framework for teaching vocabulary (see Figure 3.1). As we accelerate instruction, we must be aware of the prior vocabulary that students might be missing. Students struggle with not only the prior vocabulary but also the new words. This can be quite a lot to handle for students, and we must plan for the teaching and learning of math vocabulary among these three tiers. Tankersley (2005) noted that students benefit from hearing the words spoken correctly before they are asked to use them on their own.

Understanding vocabulary words is a complicated endeavor. Dale (1965) discusses the complexity of word knowledge, stating that it is not an "all or nothing" proposition but rather a continuum (cited in Beck et al., 2013):

Figure 3.1. Beck's Three-Tier Vocabulary Framework

Tier 1	Tier 2	Tier 3
Basic Words (words used in regular conversation but that have specific meaning in math)	**General Academic Terms** (interdisciplinary words)	**Domain-Specific Words** (math vocabulary)
in the and	justify explain compare	fraction decimal multiply rhombus
What gets really tricky here is general words that have multiple meanings, such as round, feet, table, and so forth. It is important to explain how we use the word in the discipline and in everyday life (Beck et al., 2002).	Think about the 12 power words (Bell, 2005): analyze, formulate compare, infer, contrast, predict, describe, summarize, explain, support, evaluate, trace.	Students have trouble with many math words involving measurement, fractions, and decimals: saying them ($3/2$), understanding them (one-thousandth), and not mixing them up (such as perimeter and area).

Source: Beck et al. (2013).

4 Stages of Word Knowledge

Stage 1—Never saw or heard it before

Stage 2—Heard it, but don't know what it means

Stage 3—Recognize it in a context as having something to do with _____. Familiar with the word

Stage 4—Know it well and remember it

Many researchers have studied how students learn and know about words and have theorized stages, levels, and continua of this process (Beck et al., 1987; Bravo & Cervetti, 2008; Hiebert, 2019; Nash & Snowling, 2006; Stahl & Stahl, 2004; Zwiers, 2008). Research has also found that thinking about and planning for the words to be taught helps teachers make the lesson content comprehensible for everyone, including emergent bilinguals (Harper & de Jong, 2004; Lager, 2006; Smith et al., 2012).

Teachers can use a preassessment tool similar to the one in Figure 3.2 to gain a more complete knowledge of each student's understanding than a simple request for a definition can afford. An added benefit of this kind of assessment is the metacognitive value of frequent use of a chart like this, in that it causes students to internalize the responses and consider them as they meet new words in any context.

Wesche and Paribakht (1996) have taken the continuum concept and developed a Vocabulary Knowledge Scale (VKS). Blachowicz and Fisher (2006)

Figure 3.2. Vocabulary Diagnostic Assessment

	What I Know About This Vocabulary Word Before the Lesson/Unit			
	I don't know this word; I have never seen it or heard it	I have seen this word before, and I think it means . . .	I know this word	I can use this word in a sentence; I can draw, write, or show an example
Fraction				
Numerator				
Denominator				
Multiply				
Product				

have expanded on the idea and created a chart to assess vocabulary words. Such tests are traditionally given and scored as a pretest and then as a posttest to assess growth. There is a structured scoring system, but I suggest that teachers use the test instead in a qualitative way as a check-in to see where students are in their knowledge by having them check the applicable box for each term. At the end of the unit, the same organizer can be used to remeasure their knowledge as a postcheck-in. Students can also be given simple emoji check-ins, as shown in Figure 3.3.

Another way to assess the familiarity of students with the prior and new vocabulary is to do a Vocabulary Recognition Task (VRT) (Stahl, 2008). This is a teacher-constructed yes–no task created to assess which words students

Figure 3.3. Postunit Vocabulary Check-In

	What I Know About This Vocabulary Word Now		
	 🙂	 😄	 🤔
Fraction			
Numerator			
Denominator			
Multiply			
Product			

Figure 3.4. Pre- and Postunit Vocabulary Recognition Check-In

VOCABULARY RECOGNITION TASK—FRACTIONS
(pretest and posttest)

We are getting ready to learn about multiplying fractions. Below you see a list of words. Put a circle around the words that you are able to read and are sure have something to do with fractions. Do not guess.

fraction	centimeter	numerator
difference	denominator	half hour
product	base ten	multiply

Use numbers, words, and pictures to describe any of the words you picked above.

are familiar with and which ones they are not. This test also has an elaborate grading system. I have adapted the test in several ways to use as a simple vocabulary check-in, as shown in Figure 3.4.

DIRECTLY TEACHING VOCABULARY

Jenkins et al. (1984) point out that students need around six experiences with math vocabulary before they actually own it, know it, and are able to use it. Math intervention teachers have to make a plan. Nagy and Townsend (2012) have found that direct vocabulary instruction improved student performance. The Marzano (2004) and Beck (Beck et al., 2013) approaches are summarized in Figure 3.5.

I suggest adding more 21st-century examples when doing word work. I like to use the Animotos app (animoto.com) to make a "mixtape" of the word in which the students can see several images and associations for the word in a visual, digital document. I would also show the word illustrated during the lesson and have students write down the illustrated versions in their student glossaries if they are in 2nd grade or above.

Figure 3.5. Research on Introducing Words

Marzano's Six-Step Approach to Vocabulary (2004)	Beck's Suggested Approach (Beck et al., 2013)
1. *Explain:* Students receive a student-friendly description, explanation, or example. 2. *Restate:* Students say what the word means in their own words. 3. *Show:* Students to act it out, look at pictures, explore it in a diagram, sketch it, or represent it with a symbol. 4. *Discuss:* Students continue to talk about it to make it their own. 5. *Refine and Reflect:* Students have multiple encounters with the word throughout the unit. 6. *Learning Games:* Students play vocabulary games to practice and internalize the meaning of the word.	1. Introduce the word. Say it. Have the students repeat it and discuss out aloud. 2. Say the word so students can hear it. Have them repeat it and play around with the sound, pattern, and feel of the word. 3. Give some real-life examples of the word. Show pictures, videos, actual things, and models. 4. Check for understanding by a variety of methods. Have students use the word in meaningful ways. They should be connecting it to real life. 5. Throughout the week/year, follow up with rich games and activities to practice and review the word.

My mentor Heidi Hayes Jacobs always says that we have to teach every subject like it is a foreign language. Being a language major myself (I studied French, Spanish, Japanese, and German in college), I get this. It makes complete sense. Beck et al. (2013) and Marzano (2004) both suggest the same things about the importance of presenting words in ways that students can hear them, say them, practice them, and eventually own them for themselves. This is done through ongoing daily practice throughout the week/year. Learning math vocabulary and understanding it goes far beyond words on the word wall or words introduced in a unit of study. This is a journey with lots of stops along the way.

PRACTICING VOCABULARY

Students need multiple experiences with math vocabulary before they actually "know" it. Teachers must have a strategic vocabulary plan to directly teach it every day throughout different units of study. The plan should include ways to introduce new words and practice the words learned throughout the year. Beck et al. (2013), Nagy and Townsend (2012), and Rollins (2014) report that graphic organizers, discussions, and paired collaborations work really well. Students should have an opportunity to make booklets and unpack vocabulary words with different prompts. They should get an opportunity to act out words and discuss them within talk frameworks.

Figure 3.6. Vocabulary Booklet

Vocabulary booklet by: Date:	Words you'll find in this booklet:
Vocabulary Word	**Definition**
What Does It Mean?	**Give an Example in Real Life**
Draw a Picture to Represent It	**Easy or Tricky?**

Additionally, games offer good reinforcement for vocabulary learning. In Tic-Tac-Toe (see Figure 3.11), students need to provide the definition of the word in order to put their Xs and Os in the squares. Charades forces students to think carefully about the word in order to either act it out or recognize it from another student's portrayal. Which One Doesn't Belong? is a game that encourages discussion of new words.

All the practice activities listed below serve well to reinforce vocabulary knowledge:

- Illustrating vocabulary words
- Acting out words
- Which One Doesn't Belong?
- Tic-Tac-Toe
- Bingo
- Crossword puzzles

Templates and Graphic Organizers

It is important to use some templates and graphic organizers to get students to unpack vocabulary words. We do this often in reading and writing, and we need to do it more in math. There is a great deal of research supporting the use of graphic organizers for helping students learn.

Figure 3.6 provides an example of a framework for a vocabulary booklet.

Another way to introduce and explore important words in a lesson is with the Frayer Vocabulary Practice Model (see Figure 3.7).

Figure 3.7. Frayer Vocabulary Practice Model

_____	
What does it mean?	**Give a real-life example.**
Draw a picture.	**Give a non-example.**

Fraction	
What does it mean?	**Give a real-life example.**
A fraction is a part of a whole.	They shared half of the pizza.
Draw a picture. 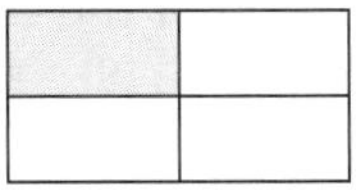	**Give a non-example.** 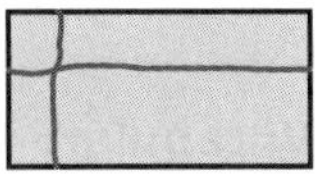

Figure 3.8. Which One Doesn't Belong?

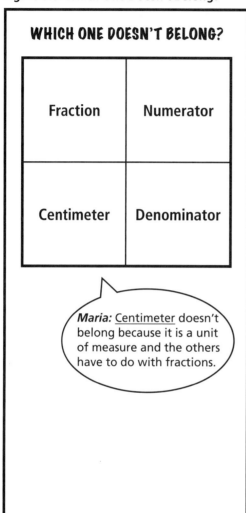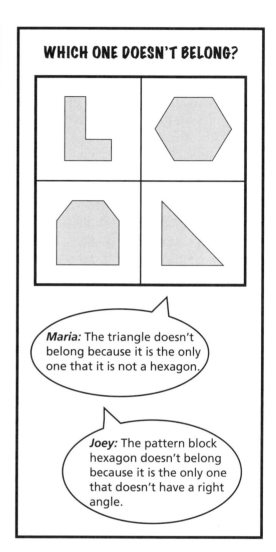

Which One Doesn't Belong?

Students love to play games. Which One Doesn't Belong? (see Figure 3.8) is a great conversation starter. Students get to discuss the four words on the game board and then decide which one they think doesn't belong and why. If done as a whole class and posted in the front, students can write their name on a Post-it and place their Post-it on the word they chose. The teacher can then facilitate a discussion of the chart.

Vocabulary Games

There are many different games that can be used to practice math vocabulary. Bingo, Tic-Tac-Toe (see Figure 3.9), crossword puzzles, and charades are great

Figure 3.9. Vocabulary Tic-Tac-Toe

VOCABULARY TIC-TAC-TOE

Partner 1:

Partner 2:

Date:

Instructions: Throw rock-paper-scissors to start the game. Whoever wins goes first. Pick a word. Circle it and write about it or draw about it on this paper. Put your initials by the word and put an X or an O on the board. Whoever gets three in a row wins.

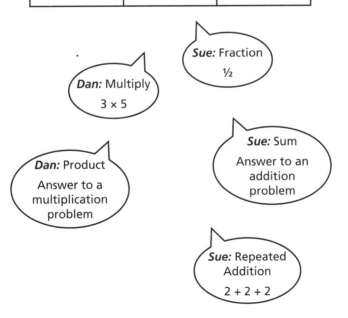

ways to practice. Several free bingo card makers are available online, where the teacher or the student can make bingo cards. Give the students Tic-Tac-Toe blank templates and have them choose nine words to play Tic-Tac-Toe. The key is that when they pick a word, they have to illustrate, draw, or write about it on the game board to prove they know it. Crossword puzzle makers are also available online (puzzlemaker.com). At first, the teacher should make puzzles for the students to use to practice the words, and then eventually the students can move on to make their own. This is a great activity because the students have to work with the vocabulary in a different way when they are creating clues for the words. Students should create their puzzles with partners.

WEAVING VOCABULARY THROUGHOUT THE LESSON

Be sure to have a word wall in the classroom and refer to the designated words on the wall throughout the lesson. Bring the words to the small group table so the students can see them. Jackson and Narvaez (2013) point out that word walls provide "visual scaffolding," and Echevarría et al. (2014) note that using visual word walls can "provide more context and 'clues' . . . because they include an illustration, definition, and sentence for each vocabulary word" (p. 81). There are many ways to display the words, as shown in Figures 3.10 and 3.11. They can be color-coded or arranged by topic. I prefer putting words from a unit of study up in a conceptual map so students can make connections between the concepts, rather than putting them up in alphabetic order.

Figure 3.10. Word Art
Word art is vocabulary words presented to look like the meaning of the word.

Figure 3.11. Math Word Wall: Definition Card

Pages for words on the word wall should include the word, an illustration, and the definition.

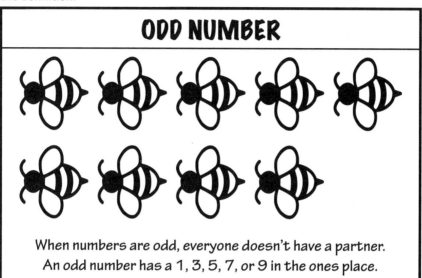

Granite School District offers wonderful premade, free, standards-based word walls and many vocabulary teaching templates (https://www.granite-schools.org/mathvocabulary/). Keystone Area Education Agency is a great source for math graphic organizer examples (https://www.keystoneaea.org/classroom-support/math/ell-math-vocabulary).

SUMMARY

Any rich math intervention program is going to have a strategic vocabulary building component built into it. Students who have been working with an accelerated model have many advantages to help them succeed. They get to do the following:

- Discuss how they would use this math in the real world
- Learn the vocabulary and use it in context
- Work with the prior vocabulary they need to know to access the content
- Connect the new vocabulary to words they already know

Acceleration impacts student motivation, self-efficacy, engagement, confidence, and participation. In accelerated lessons, students feel safe, and they will take risks. In such a risk-taking environment, students will succeed and thrive.

CHAPTER 4

Acceleration Lesson Plan Format

Acceleration jump-starts underperforming students into learning new concepts before their classmates even begin. Rather than being stuck in the remedial slow lane, students move ahead of everyone into the fast lane of learning. Acceleration provides a fresh academic start for students every week and creates opportunities for struggling students to learn alongside their more successful peers.

—Rollins (2014)

INSTRUCTION PLAN

Acceleration starts with careful planning. Many districts and states offer sample acceleration lesson plans. The Texas Education Agency, for example, hosts a number of acceleration resources on its website (https://tea.texas.gov/texas-schools/health-safety-discipline/covid/accelerated-learning-resources). Check to see what resources and support are available to you in your school, district, and state.

Figure 4.1 provides a sample template for planning the acceleration process for an individual student; the form can be adapted for a group. (All figures for this chapter are grouped at the end of the chapter.)

When. How often will you do the acceleration meetings? Research says that it should be at least 3 times a week for 30 minutes each. The reality, though, is that you have to work within your schedule. Many schools do it during the school day. Acceleration is a separate time from regular math class. It should not be done during core math instruction. Many schools have a time set aside every day for math intervention and math enrichment. Other schools have someone push into the classroom at some point in the day to pull aside small acceleration groups. Some schools do acceleration before or after school.

Where. Where will the math intervention take place? Will it be inside the core classroom during instruction as a pull-aside group? Will it be outside the core classroom in a designated room for math intervention? In general, research recommends that push-in programs work better than pull-out programs. Also, math intervention should be in addition to, not instead of, core math class. All students should be present for the core instruction and actively participate in that work. In addition to the core instruction, those who need it should receive the math intervention.

Who. A variety of people can conduct the accelerated lessons. Research says that it is best when the core classroom teacher or an instructional assistant does it. Either of these people should be paid (if instruction is done outside of regular working hours) and trained in how to accelerate learning. The easiest way is to have the core classroom teacher lead the lessons because they already know what they need to know to do the intervention. If another teacher or an instructional assistant does the intervention, then it is important to make sure that those teachers get all the information they need to make the intervention work. There can also be other people who participate, such as a parent, volunteer, or other paid professional (such as one from AmeriCorps or another service organization). In all cases, these people should be paid and trained.

Time. Schools do lots of different things to reach and teach all their students. Some offer before-school programs. Others have after-school programs. Others do acceleration sometime during the school day. Some schools will have an extra teacher come in during some part of the class (preferably not during math class) and pull aside groups. Sometimes the acceleration takes place during math time after the main lesson, when students are doing independent work. Other schools do before- and after-school tutoring programs or even Saturday school. Some schools have extended the school day so they have time to add an extended learning time program.

ASSESSMENT PLAN

It is important to consider how you will assess along the way. Use a variety of ways, including quick quizzes, exit slips, artifacts of student work, written and verbal reflections, and quick mini-interviews. Be sure to collect something every day to monitor progress. Think about how you will use this information to guide the next instructional steps. Will you go over the information with the students or their parents, or will you develop it with the classroom teacher if you are a tutor? How will you share this information in a way that motivates students and helps them succeed? Planning tools such as those shown in Figures 4.2 and 4.3 can be helpful.

PROGRESS MONITORING

The data you collect will tell you what the next instructional move should be. Is the student making progress? Are they staying the same? Are they going down? Do you need to change what you are doing or keep doing the same thing? The data give guidance in answering all these questions. When using the form in Figure 4.3, answer 100%, 75%, or Not Yet. The reality is that if you are doing an intervention and the student hasn't quite grasped the material yet, you need to keep working on the concept for a few weeks before deciding to change course. You also want to consider the student's affect. How are they doing? Are they engaged, apathetic, encouraged, or hopeless? These states of mind have a major impact on how the intervention is going too. How will affect play a role in your instructional decisions? How will you address the situation?

KEEPING TRACK THROUGHOUT THE LESSON

Anecdotal notes (see Figures 4.4A, 4.4B, and 4.5) help us keep a record of what is happening in the moment. They inform what happens next. Remember that anything a student does is part of the evidence of the journey. How they act, what they say, what they do and do not do, how they feel, what they emote—all these things give us needed information about how they are processing the information, taking it in, and learning it. Are you recording and catching it all so that you will know exactly what to do next to ensure they are successful?

Figure 4.5 shows another type of recording sheet for tracking progress throughout the journey. This particular sheet captures the preassessment, the ongoing assessments, and the postassessment. It can give a good snapshot of the intervention.

PLANNING CHECKLISTS

Planning checklists like the one in Figure 4.6 help teachers to quickly think about all the elements of the intervention. What does the launch look like? What prior knowledge will the teacher be connecting to? How will that connection take place? What will the progress monitoring look like specifically? What type of feedback will be given, when, and how? What is the role of student reflection throughout the process?

REFLECTING ON THE ACCELERATION PROCESS

It is also important to think about the overall assessment process. In what ways are you collecting evidence of learning along the way? What are you doing with that information? Does it encourage or discourage the student? Do they feel motivated to keep trying after having had a conversation with you about their progress? Stiggins (2007) states very emphatically that this is what assessment information should be doing: It should be encouraging students, letting them know where they are and where they are going, and affirming that through hard work and perseverance they can get there. Figure 4.7 offers a format for thinking about important evaluation questions.

SUMMARY

A well-designed accelerated intervention program starts long before the actual intervention ever begins. It takes planning, planning, and more planning. It also takes flexibility, because the best laid plans need to be adjusted when the students get there. We always have to consider a few essential questions:

1. What do the students need?
2. Is what I have preplanned working?
3. Do I need to shift gears? Why and how?
4. How do the students feel? How is that impacting their engagement? What is my next move?
5. What can I do to make sure everybody is accessing this content?

Figures 4.1–4.7 appear on pages 41–48.

Figure 4.1. Accelerated Instruction Plan

INSTRUCTION PLAN

Date:

Student:

Subject:

Teacher:

I. Acceleration Learning Plan (or see attached documentation for the standards)

Current Grade-Level Standard:	**Prior Grade-Level Standard:**
Knowledge and Skills Needed:	**Knowledge and Skills Needed:**

Acceleration Plan:

What will you specifically review?

- How will you bridge the connections?

- How will you scaffold the learning?

Students could meet this new standard if they just knew:

Vocabulary:

Sentence Frames:

Manipulatives:

Templates:

II. Logistics

When: Frequency	☐ 2 times a week ☐ 3 times a week ☐ _____ times a week
Where: Location	☐ In class ☐ In other teacher's room
Who: Who will do the math intervention?	☐ Classroom teacher ☐ Another teacher ☐ Instructional assistant ☐ Parent ☐ Volunteer ☐ Other (paid professional/fellow)
Time:	☐ During school ☐ Before school ☐ After school ☐ Push-in ☐ Pull-out ☐ Part of regular program ☐ 20 minutes ☐ 30 minutes ☐ Other (minutes)

Figure 4.2. Making an Overall Assessment Plan

ASSESSMENT PLAN
1. What data will you use for progress monitoring?
2. How often will you monitor progress?
3. How will the students be involved in the process?
4. How will families be involved in the process?
5. What will the artifacts/evidence look like?

Assessment Instrument Options

Test 1	☐ Quiz	☐ Artifact of the work	☐ Student reflection	☐ Quick interview
Test 2	☐ Quiz	☐ Artifact of the work	☐ Student reflection	☐ Quick interview
Test 3	☐ Quiz	☐ Artifact of the work	☐ Student reflection	☐ Quick interview
Test 4	☐ Quiz	☐ Artifact of the work	☐ Student reflection	☐ Quick interview

What are the success criteria?

Figure 4.3. Monitoring Progress

Weekly Progress Monitoring	Present, Absent, Other	Progress		Student Affect	
		☐ 100% ☐ Not Yet	☐ 75%	☐ Motivated ☐ Other	☐ Frustrated
		☐ 100% ☐ Not Yet	☐ 75%	☐ Motivated ☐ Other	☐ Frustrated
		☐ 100% ☐ Not Yet	☐ 75%	☐ Motivated ☐ Other	☐ Frustrated
		☐ 100% ☐ Not Yet	☐ 75%	☐ Motivated ☐ Other	☐ Frustrated
		☐ 100% ☐ Not Yet	☐ 75%	☐ Motivated ☐ Other	☐ Frustrated
		☐ 100% ☐ Not Yet	☐ 75%	☐ Motivated ☐ Other	☐ Frustrated
		☐ 100% ☐ Not Yet	☐ 75%	☐ Motivated ☐ Other	☐ Frustrated
		☐ 100% ☐ Not Yet	☐ 75%	☐ Motivated ☐ Other	☐ Frustrated
		☐ 100% ☐ Not Yet	☐ 75%	☐ Motivated ☐ Other	☐ Frustrated
		☐ 100% ☐ Not Yet	☐ 75%	☐ Motivated ☐ Other	☐ Frustrated

Figure 4.4A. Anecdotal Notes for a Group

ANECDOTAL NOTES		
Group: **Topic:** **Teacher:** **Date:**		
Group:	Who has learned it? Who is progressing? Who is still beginning to learn the topic? What is the affect of the group toward this topic? What is the affect of the group toward each other?	What will the follow-up be?
Observations, Noticings, Wonderings		
Date: **Group:** What happened? What will you do next?	**Date:** **Group:** What happened? What will you do next?	**Date:** **Group:** What happened? What will you do next?

Figure 4.4B. Anecdotal Notes for an Individual Student

ANECDOTAL NOTES
Student Name: **Topic:** **Teacher:** **Date:**
What did you notice? • Strengths   • Challenges
What do you wonder? • Strengths   • Challenges
What should you do next?

Figure 4.5. Student Progress Monitoring

STUDENT PROGRESS MONITORING

Name:

Grade:

Acceleration Topic:

Preassessment Information

Ongoing Assessment Information	
Dates	Notes

Summative Assessment Information

What are the next steps?

Aha moments:

Any changes?

Other comments:

Figure 4.6. Accelerated Math Lesson Checklist

Stage	Topic/Activity
Clear Learning Goal	
Success Criteria	
Engaging Launch	
Vocabulary	
Review of Prior Content Skills Needed for This Concept	
Connection to Current Content	
Progress Monitoring	
Feedback	
Student Check-In/Self-Reflection	

Figure 4.7. Evaluating Acceleration: Reflection Activity

Reflection Question	Response
What lessons did you do this week?	
Why did you choose those lessons?	
How did you engage the students throughout the lessons?	
How did you check for understanding throughout the lessons?	
What kind of guided practice did you give the students?	
How do you know they learned the concepts?	
What is the evidence of learning?	
How did you incorporate academic language throughout the lessons?	
What went really well?	
Would you do anything differently next time? Why or why not?	
Do you have anything else to add?	

CHAPTER 5

Acceleration and Pedagogy

> The more ways something is learned, the more memory pathways are built.
> This brain research discovery is part of the reason for the current notion that
> stimulating the growth of more dendrites and synaptic connections is one of the
> best things teachers can learn to do for the brains of their students.
>
> —Willis (2006)

Standards-based, academically rigorous, culturally affirming and sustaining, and engaging grade-level teaching can provide a solid foundation for all students to learn math. But sometimes some students need a little extra help, beyond the core instruction. This help should be provided in a way that supports students to access the grade-level curriculum (Baldwin et al., 2021). All students can learn and should be given the opportunity to learn with a rich, relevant, rigorous curriculum in a loving environment and with knowledgeable teachers who believe in them.

The teaching of an acceleration group must be engaging and enthralling, and it must spark curiosity. We learn more when we are interested in what is being taught. We learn more when we see the relevance of the matter to our real lives. We learn more when we engage in a variety of forms of practice. In education, as we provide practice in ways that interest and make sense to students, we stimulate formation of multiple brain pathways, which helps strengthen their long-term memory (Willis, 2006). We should be doing memorable things during the lesson so that students will retain what they are learning by making connections to past learning and personal experiences and having a positive emotional state of mind.

Multisensory experiences are very important. We should be tapping into learning preferences and multiple ways of teaching and learning so that we can reach all learners. Willis (2006) points out that the more ways students wrestle with a topic, the more they are "stimulating multiple sensory intake center in their brains. Their brains develop multiple pathways leading to the same memory storage destination." This means that they have several different ways to recall and retrieve that knowledge. If you have done several things to stimulate learning on a topic, then students will be better able to visualize the information, make meaning from personal experience, act out the situation, and create products related to the math.

Our brains try to make sense of new data by connecting it to older information. We should start each lesson by engaging the students. Researchers note that we need to grab students' attention before the new information can be taken in. We need to tap into "novelty, humor and surprise," among other things, to engage and capture attentive focus so that we can get new information into the memory circuits (Koutstaal et al., 1997; Willis, 2006).

RECOMMENDATIONS FOR MATHEMATICAL INTERVENTION

As teachers are planning accelerated lessons, we must draw on the intervention research. The Institute of Education Sciences (IES) is conducting a rigorous, long-term review of research reports on mathematical intervention practices in the elementary and middle school grades. Eight recommendations have arisen out of these analyses (IES, 2009; see Figure 5.1):

Figure 5.1. Research-Supported Intervention Recommendations

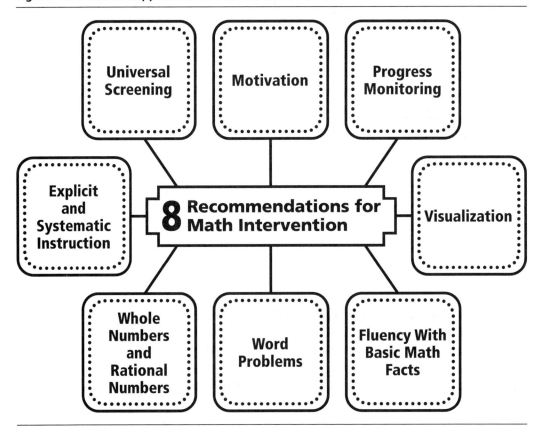

1. Conduct universal screening to identify students who might be at risk.
2. Focus on student learning in whole numbers for Grades K–4 and in rational numbers for Grades 4–8 (after whole numbers have been mastered).
3. Focus on explicit and systematic instruction during the intervention lessons.
4. Teach students how to unpack word problems so that they may recognize mathematical structure as they work through them.
5. Focus on visualization.
6. Devote at least 10 minutes a day to increasing fluency with math facts.
7. Conduct ongoing progress monitoring throughout the process.
8. Develop productive methods for motivating students throughout the intervention in a way that impacts their mathematical disposition for life.

Several of the IES (2009) recommendations are discussed in this chapter. Chapters 6, 7, and 8 provide lesson examples of acceleration focusing on whole numbers and rational numbers. Progress monitoring was covered in Chapter 4, and we will discuss motivation in depth in Chapter 9.

EXPLICIT AND SYSTEMATIC INSTRUCTION

Math intervention lessons can be approached in various ways, but research suggests that we use explicit and systematic instruction at Tiers 2 and 3. Importantly, Rosenshine (1987) described explicit instruction as "a systematic method of teaching with emphasis on proceeding in small steps, checking for understanding, and achieving active and successful participation by all students." Too often, explicit instruction is misunderstood and written about as teacher-driven and a space where students are passive.

Hattie (2018) reports that the effect size for direct instruction is 0.59, which reflects a strong influence. Almarode and Piccininni (2019) point out that the characteristics that Hattie is referring to are very different from how many people perceive explicit instruction. Hattie is talking about a practice where the teachers make the learning goals and success criteria explicit and accessible so that all learners know what they are studying, why it is important, and what it looks like when they are successful. Almarode and Piccininni note that students

- are actively involved in the lesson,
- know what they are learning, and
- always wrap it up and talk about the takeaways at the end of the lesson.

Formative assessment is an integral part of the learning journey, and both teachers and students are involved in looking at and analyzing these assessments to see what they say about the learner's progress and what the next steps are. The lessons are interactive, and teachers engage students in an ongoing cycle of modeling, demonstration, guided practice, and feedback. Almarode and Piccininni (2019) also mention that teachers should be using exemplars and examples. Fischer et al. (2021) point out that it is also very important for students to experience "early and small wins" along the way (p. 53).

Math Intervention Lesson

The cycle for an intervention lesson includes the elements shown in Figure 5.2.

Figure 5.2. Intervention Lesson Path

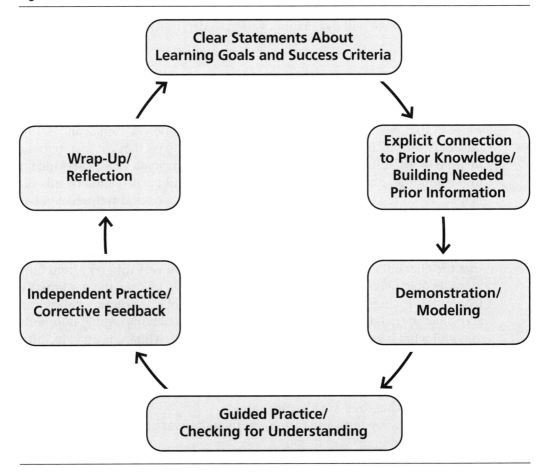

"Using high-quality corrective instruction is not the same as reteaching, which often con-sists simply of restating the original explanations louder and more slowly. Instead, the teacher must use approaches that accommodate differences in students' learning styles . . . (Sternberg, 1994). Although teachers generally try to incorporate different approaches when they plan their lessons, corrective instruction extends and strengthens that work."

—Guskey (2007)

Distributed and Deliberate Practice

Chapters 6, 7, and 8 provide a few pages of scaffolds that include ways for students to practice. Intentional targeted practice is a very important part of learning. Francisco (2019) points out that distributed practice across the year is vital. Students need the ongoing practice year-round, and not simply just in the massed practice sessions they get during a particular unit of study. This is one of the reasons why we work on math fluency for 10 minutes at the begin-ning or end of every lesson (IES, 2009). And it is also why we have activities like Whole Number of the Day, Fraction of the Day, or Decimal of the Day (not done every day but practiced every week)—so that students can work on these hot topics all year long. In these activities, students review the designat-ed topic by adding, subtracting, multiplying, or dividing the designated num-bers, depending on the grade. The scaffolding materials at the ends of Chapters 6, 7, and 8 include examples of flashcards, board games, posters, and more that students can use not only to support their initial learning but also to engage in distributed practice across the year.

Accelerating instruction is also built around the idea of deliberate practice (Almarode et al., 2021; Ericsson, 2016; Lehtinen et al., 2017). This is not a drill-and-kill approach. This is intentional, focused, cognitively demanding work that students engage with over time, focusing on targeted and specific goals guided by a teacher, coach, or tutor. Feedback is a crucial part of the process. In the beginning of the process, teachers give a great deal of feed-back, but eventually the student learns to self-monitor. Deliberate practice is about doing the work, reflecting on the process, modifying and improving, and cycling through the routine over and over again. Deliberate practice re-quires that students are actively involved in the process throughout.

VISUALIZATION

Visualization is an essential part of teaching math acceleration lessons. Boonen et al. (2014) found that "compared to students who did not make a visual representation, those who produced an accurate visual-schematic representation increased the chance of solving a word problem correctly almost six times." However, they also found that inaccurate representations

Figure 5.3. Three Forms of Visualization to Support Learning

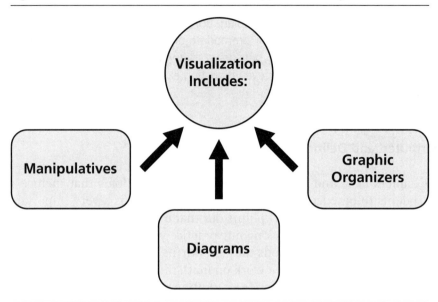

"decreased . . . [the] chance of success" (p. 1). Teachers must know how, when, and why to use visual representations with students. Visual representation is "more than simply a picture or detailed illustration. . . . Often referred to as a *schematic representation* or *schematic diagram*[, it] is an accurate depiction of a given problem's mathematical quantities and relationships" (IRIS Center, 2022). Visual representations help scaffold understanding. They help students "see the math" that they are doing. They help students comprehend the math and make connections between the concrete, pictorial, and abstract representations of the topic. Visualization includes manipulatives, diagrams, and graphic organizers, as shown in Figure 5.3.

Manipulatives

Accelerated lessons should go through a cycle of concrete, pictorial, and abstract. Oftentimes, upper elementary and middle school teachers do not use manipulatives enough! We must build conceptual understanding through concrete representations of these tricky, complex topics. Once there is understanding, the manipulatives can be phased out. Build it, draw it, explain it, and represent it symbolically. In the primary grades we need rekenreks, number paths, beaded number lines, and hundred grids. In the upper elementary grades and middle school, we should be using beaded number lines, integer number lines, algebra tiles, percent squares, decimal wheels and grids, and fraction bars, squares, and circles. It is imperative that we use manipulatives to build understanding. The variety of these aids can be seen in Figure 5.4.

When using manipulatives, it is important to

- make explicit connections between the concrete object, the pictorial representation, and the abstract concept (it is not a hierarchy),
- remember that teacher questioning is key—manipulatives aren't magic on their own, and
- make sure that students are talking about and explaining the math they are working on.

Diagrams and Graphic Organizers

We understand that visualization is important (Zhang et al., 2012), and diagrams and graphic organizers are another way to help us organize and reason about information (Dexter & Hughes, 2011; Zollman, 2009). Diagrams can help with problem solving (Glazebrook, 2015), and they can help us look at the relationships between objects, concepts, and facts. Graphic organizers can help us convert information from text form into an eye-catching and readily assimilated visual form. They can help us detect patterns.

Diagrams and graphic organizers can help us organize information, visualize it, and then think about and discuss it. In math classrooms the teacher should not be the only one asking questions. The students should be able to

Figure 5.4. Manipulatives by Grade Band

	Tools Every Classroom Needs
Primary Grades	• 10-, 20-, and 100-beaded number lines • Rekenreks (20 and 100 beads) • Number paths, number lines, hundred grids • Number bonds • Place-value blocks, place-value disks
Upper Elementary Grades	• 10-, 20-, and 100-beaded number lines • Base-ten blocks • Fraction tiles, fraction circles, fraction squares • Decimal hundredth grid, decimal number line • Decimal tiles, percent tiles
Middle Grades	• Beaded number lines • Integer beaded and paper number lines • Fraction tiles • Algebra tiles • Decimal tiles, percent tiles

come up with observations and questions too. Diagrams and graphic organizers can help them do that.

Various templates and tools for creating diagrams and graphic organizers are widely available, and as we employ them we must understand that we want students to use both internal and external representations (Matheson & Hutchinson, 2020). We have to teach students how to internalize visualizations so that they can easily reference them when doing math (see, e.g., Figure 5.5).

Figure 5.5. Number Bonds

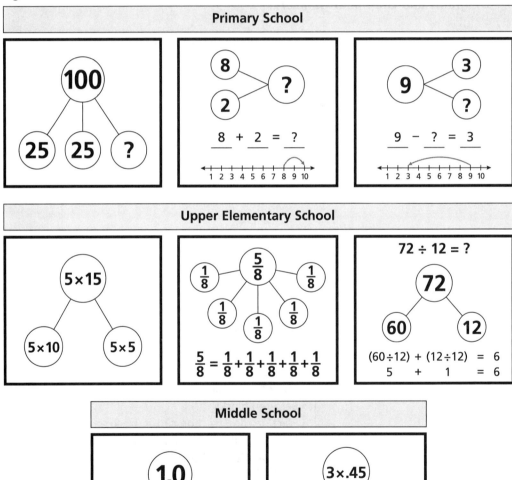

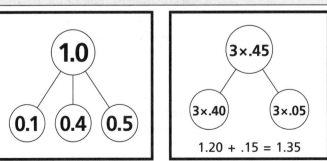

Some Useful Visual Tools

Visual Displays. Visual displays are used for showing spatial relationships and can perform a number of specific functions. Venn diagrams, for example, can be used to make comparisons between objects or concepts (see Figure 5.6). A timeline can display information temporally, which could be helpful in solving a word problem.

Number Paths and Number Lines. The number line diagram is an essential part of all math learning. Number lines like those shown in Figure 5.7 help students see numbers in a sequence—in time and in space. They can talk about, explain, compare, and calculate numbers presented in this context. With support of the number line, students begin to internalize the things they can do, and eventually they are able to work without the external representation.

WORD PROBLEMS

The Institute of Education Sciences (2009) states that unpacking word problems and understanding their structure is an important part of math intervention. Throughout accelerated lessons, teachers should present, discuss, teach, unpack, model, demonstrate, and encourage students to wrestle with and persevere through word problems.

State and national high-stakes assessments require that students demonstrate proficiency in solving word problems, yet many students face significant challenges in doing so. Emergent bilinguals wrestle with the language.

Figure 5.6. Venn Diagram: Multiples of 3, Multiples of 5, and Multiples of Both

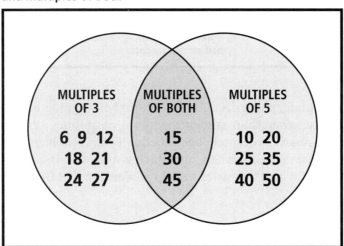

Figure 5.7. Number Paths and Number Lines

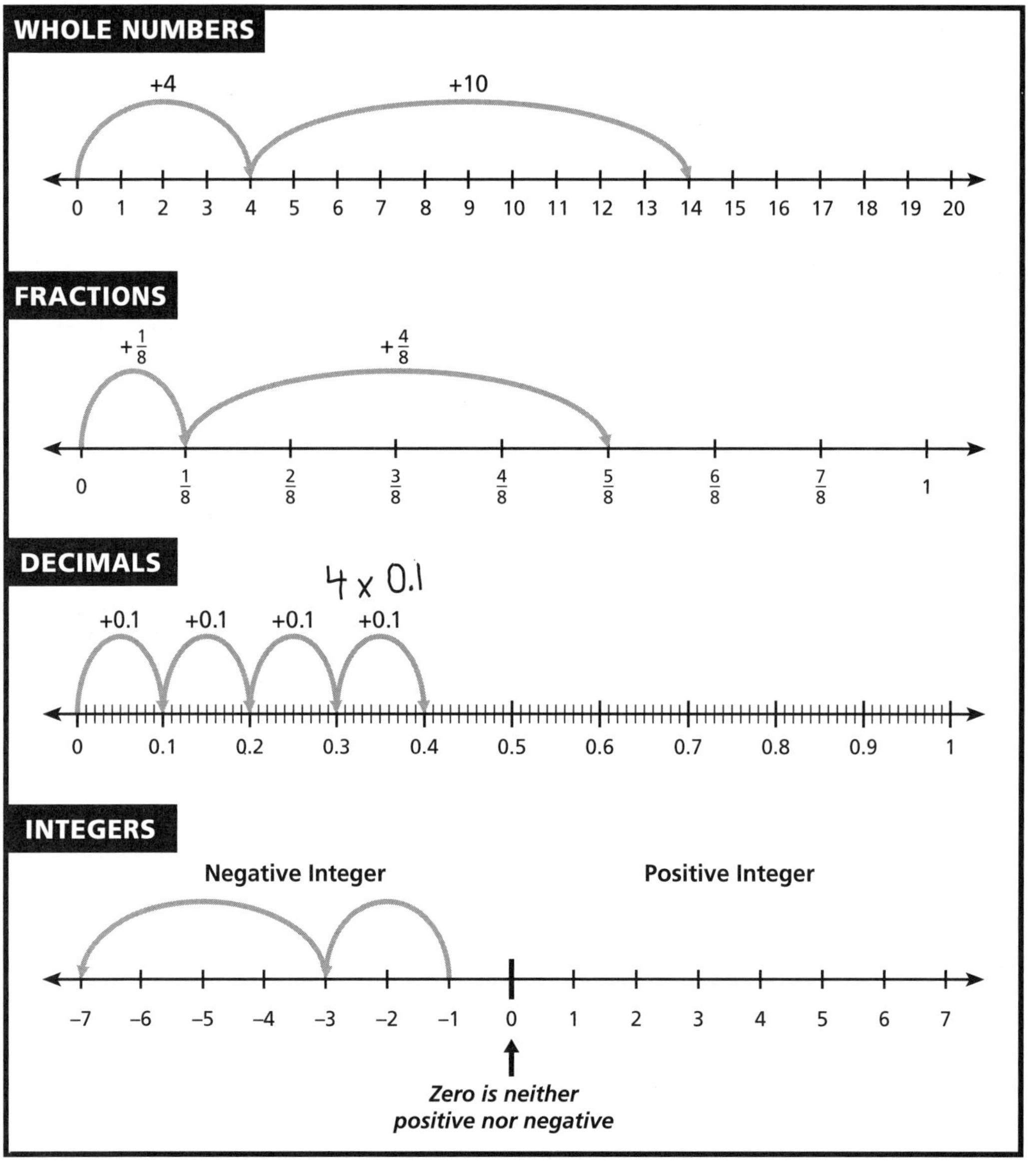

Students with learning disabilities perform below grade-level proficiency and significantly lower than students without disabilities (Powell et al., 2017). But, really, nearly everybody needs help. Do word problems every day. Set up real-life story contexts when introducing and working through math concepts. Use tools and templates to help students model their thinking.

Types of Word Problems

Most state standards take a schema-based approach to word problems and designate different types of word problems to solve at specific grade levels. The types of problems students are expected to handle increase in complexity by the grade. Cognitively Guided Instruction (CGI) (Carpenter et al., 1999/ 2014) has helped to make schema-based problem solving doable. Figures 5.8A and 5.8B show the different types of CGI word problems students are typically responsible for from kindergarten through 2nd grade and from 3rd through 5th grades.

Visuals for Word Problems

Part-part-whole mats and tape diagrams are great for modeling math problems because they give students a way of thinking about and organizing the numbers they are working with. For example, Figure 5.9 shows how students can place the known and figure out where the unknown goes. They might say, We had 5 blue marbles and 4 green ones. How many did we have altogether? Students can see that they know both parts and they are looking for the whole. The graphic organizer gives them a way to think about what is known and what is unknown.

Figure 5.10 shows how tape diagrams can create a visual scaffold for students to unpack and understand the multiplicative comparison word problem. Students might build this problem first with Cuisenaire rods™ and then draw it out. For the Upper Elementary example, they would put down a 5 rod and then 3 times as many; with the tools and the diagram they can see what that actually means. With the visualization of the problem, students can answer many questions—many more than they would have been able to answer without the visualization. For example, how many more does Sue's sister have than she does? How many do they have altogether? How many more would Sue need to have as many as her sister?

GRAPHIC ORGANIZERS

Research shows that graphic organizers are quite effective in improving achievement in mathematics by helping students to organize information, analyze relationships, and visually unpack ideas and vocabulary (Dexter & Hughes, 2011; Strangman et al., 2004; Zollman, 2009). Graphic organizers help students with "mapping cause and effect, note taking, comparing and contrasting concepts, organizing problems and solutions, [and] relating information," among other things (Strangman et al., 2004, p. 6). Graphic organizers help students organize information in a way that allows them to quickly see the concepts and break apart and map out the components of a topic.

Figure 5.8A. Word Problem Types: Kindergarten–Grade 2

INTRODUCTION TO THE TYPES OF PROBLEMS			
Join/ Separate	**Result Unknown**	**Change Unknown**	**Start Unknown**
Join	Marta had 5 marbles. She got 2 more. How many does she have now? • 5 + 2 = ?	Marta had 5 marbles. She got some more. Now she has 7. How many did she get? • 5 + ? = 7 *or* • 7 − 5 = ?	Marta had some marbles. She got 2 more. Now she has 5. How many did she have in the beginning? • ? + 2 = 5
Separate	Joe had 10 marbles. He gave 2 to his brother. How many does he have left? • 10 − 2 = ?	Joe has 10 marbles. He gave some to his friends. Now he has 5 left. How many did he give away? • 10 − ? = 5	Joe had some marbles. He gave 3 away. Now he has 7. How many did he have in the beginning? • ? − 3 = 7 or • 3 + 7 = ?
Part-Part-Whole	**Whole Unknown**	**Both Addends Unknown**	**Part Unknown**
Part-Part-Whole	Jamal had 3 big marbles and 4 small marbles. How many did he have altogether? • 3 + 4 = 7	Jamal had 7 marbles. Some were big and some were small. How many of each could he have? • 7 + 0; 6 + 1; 5 + 2; 4 + 3; 3 + 4; 2 + 5; 1 + 6; 0 + 7	Jamal had 7 marbles. 3 were big. The rest were small. How many were small? • 7 − 3 = ? • 3 + ? = 7
Compare	**Difference** (easy version)	**Bigger Part Unknown** (easy version)	**Smaller Part Unknown** (easy version)
Compare	Grace had 7 rings. Lucy had 4. How many more rings did Grace have than Lucy? • 7 − 4 = ? • 4 + ? = 7	Lucy had 4 rings. Grace had 3 more than she did. How many did Grace have? • 4 + 3 = ?	Grace had 7 rings. Lucy had 3 fewer than she did. How many did Lucy have? • 7 − 3 = ?
Compare	**Difference** (harder version)	**Bigger Part Unknown** (harder version)	**Smaller Part Unknown** (harder version)
Compare	Grace had 7 rings. Lucy had 4. How many fewer rings did Lucy have than Grace? • 7 − 4 = ?	Lucy had 4 rings. She had 3 fewer than Grace. How many did Grace have? • ? − 3 = 4 or • 4 + 3 = ?	Grace had 7 rings. She had 3 more than Lucy. How many did Lucy have? • 7 − 3 = ?

Figure 5.8B. Word Problem Types: Grades 3–5

CGI MULTIPLICATION AND DIVISION PROBLEMS			
	Unknown Product	**Group Size Unknown**	**Number of Groups Unknown**
Equal Groups	There are 4 boxes with 5 donuts in each box. How many donuts are there altogether?	If 20 donuts are put equally into 4 boxes, then how many donuts will be in each box?	If there are 20 donuts and the bakery puts 5 in a box, how many boxes are there?
Arrays/Area	There are 3 rows of orange trees with 5 trees in each row. How many trees are there in total?	There are 15 trees. They are equally divided into 3 rows. How many are in each row?	There are 15 trees. There are 5 in each row. How many rows are there?
Compare	Mary has 5 marbles. Her sister has 2 times as many as she does. How many does her sister have?	Jamal has 9 marbles. He has 3 times as many as his brother. How many does his brother have?	Grace has 10 marbles. Kim has 2 marbles. How many times as many marbles does Grace have as Kim?

Figure 5.9. Part-Part-Whole Models and an Example of a Workmat

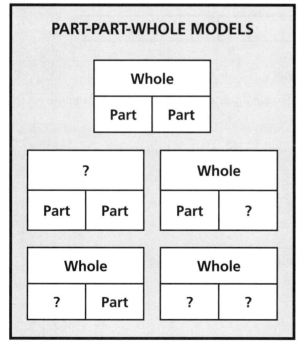
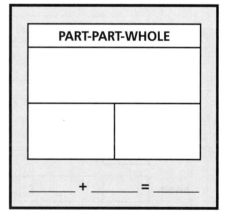

Graphic Organizers in the Classroom

There are many different types of graphic organizers. A wide variety of templates are readily available online, and teacher instruction in their effective implementation plays a key role in successful classroom use (Merkley & Jefferies, 2001). Teachers are strongly encouraged to use graphic organizers as an integral part of their accelerated lessons.

Two examples highlight the usefulness of graphic organizers in the classroom. The Frayer model is an easily used tool for vocabulary building (see

Figure 5.10. Tape Diagrams

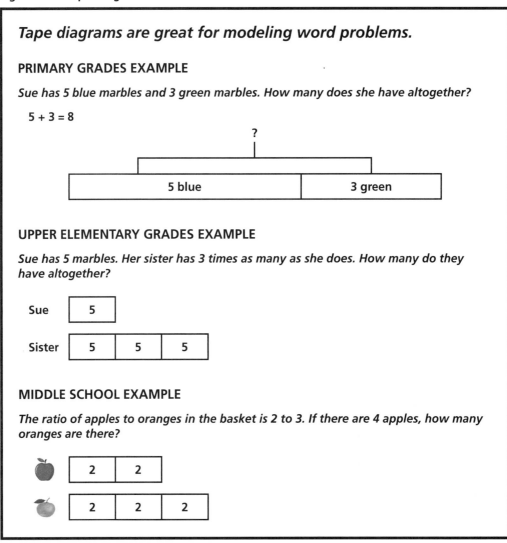

Tape diagrams are great for modeling word problems.

PRIMARY GRADES EXAMPLE

Sue has 5 blue marbles and 3 green marbles. How many does she have altogether?

$5 + 3 = 8$

5 blue	3 green

UPPER ELEMENTARY GRADES EXAMPLE

Sue has 5 marbles. Her sister has 3 times as many as she does. How many do they have altogether?

Sue | 5 |

Sister | 5 | 5 | 5 |

MIDDLE SCHOOL EXAMPLE

The ratio of apples to oranges in the basket is 2 to 3. If there are 4 apples, how many oranges are there?

| 2 | 2 |

| 2 | 2 | 2 |

Figure 5.11. Frayer Model: A Tool for Building Vocabulary

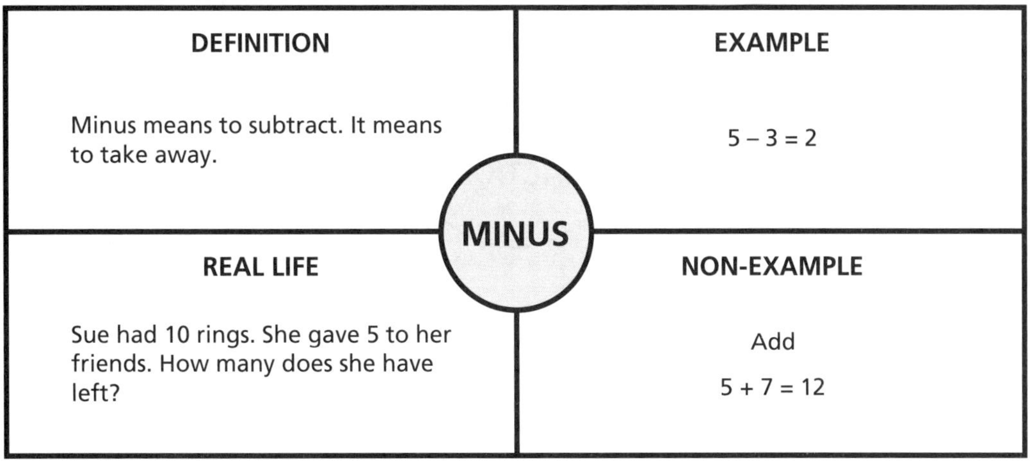

DEFINITION	EXAMPLE
Minus means to subtract. It means to take away.	$5 - 3 = 2$
REAL LIFE	NON-EXAMPLE
Sue had 10 rings. She gave 5 to her friends. How many does she have left?	Add $5 + 7 = 12$

MINUS

Figure 5.11). Completed Frayer organizers can be retained for use as resources in future work and as tools for review. Semantic maps (or webs) are useful for graphically displaying the connections between words or concepts (see Figure 5.12). Among many other purposes, they can be used to activate prior knowledge and to build vocabulary. The mind map is a form of semantic map.

Choosing the Best Graphic Organizers

As teachers are preparing for a cycle of acceleration, they must ask themselves a series of questions about the tools and templates they are using. Tools don't just inherently teach, teachers must plan experiences that connect mathematical ideas with the tools and give students opportunities to explore and understand through doing. Here are some sample questions to ask as students work with tools:

- What are you trying to do?
- How do you need to break down the concepts and skill steps so that students understand what they are doing?
- Which graphic organizer best helps to unpack, analyze, discuss, and ultimately understand that information?
- How does the manipulative, organizer, or diagram help you do that?
- How will you introduce it?

BUILDING MATHEMATICAL PROFICIENCY

The focus during an acceleration cycle is getting all students to be mathematically proficient. Thus, the reason for the work is much more than simply

Figure 5.12. Semantic Map: A Way to Display Connections

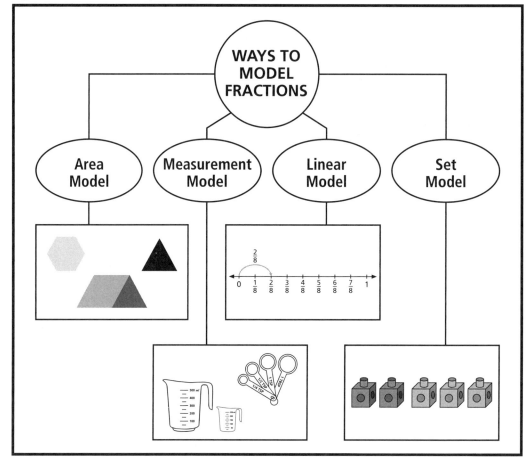

teaching students how to get an answer. There are five components of mathematical proficiency: conceptual understanding, procedural fluency, adaptive reasoning, strategic competence, and adaptive disposition (National Research Council, 2001; see Figure 5.13). We want students to understand the concepts of the math they are doing and to understand how to do it. We also want students to be able to reason out loud about what they are doing. They should be able to explain, defend, prove, and justify the steps they are taking. They need to be able to think flexibly and to know more than one way to reach a goal. We also want students to be confident, competent, curious learners.

Fluency in Math Facts

Research on math intervention reveals that we focus on building fluency in math facts at least 10 minutes each day. Basic fact fluency is a superpower. All students need it. Students need to practice facts in ways that build flexibility,

Figure 5.13. Five Elements of Mathematical Proficiency

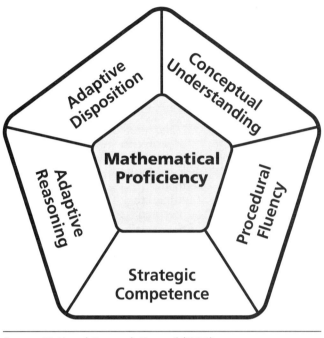

Source: National Research Council (2001).

accuracy, and efficiency. This takes targeted, intentional, distributed practice across the year. Some of this work will be done in the school, and other parts will have to be done at home. The work should be scaffolded so that students make meaningful connections throughout the process. The focus should be on building strategic competence. All students can learn their math facts with a scaffolded learning trajectory, time, and perseverance.

Mathematical Practices and Processes

Throughout accelerated lessons we are focusing on mathematical practices as well as the mechanics of performing specific operations. In building proficiency in math, the practices and thought processes emphasized are just as important as the math content itself (National Council of Teachers of Mathematics [NCTM], 2000; National Governors Association Center for Best Practices & Council of Chief State School Officers [NGA & CCSSO], 2010). NCTM (2000) has identified five broad types of processes in the performance of math: problem solving, reasoning and proof, communication, connections, and representation. Other national organizations and individual states have developed more detailed listings of mathematical practices, but there is a good deal of overlap with the NCTM (2010) processes. Eight math practices

Figure 5.14. Mathematical Practices

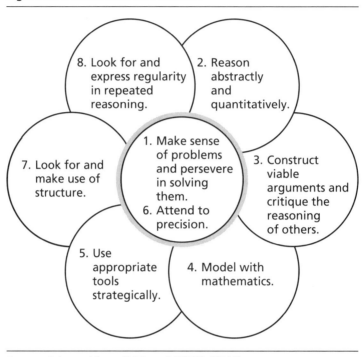

Source: Adapted from NGA and CCSSO (2010).

commonly incorporated into specific sets of standards are shown in Figure 5.14. Whichever standard we might be following, in teaching our students we are trying to get them to do several things. We want them to persevere in solving problems, reason abstractly and quantitatively, communicate what they are doing, model their thinking, use tools, attend to precision, understand the structure of numbers, and recognize, use, and discuss patterns.

MATH TALK

Math Think Alouds

It is important to do math think alouds with students. Teachers need to engage students in talking through math. Krawec et al. (2013) discuss how it is really important for students to verbalize what they are thinking and seeing in their mind and then learn to draw those images. Use of visualization is an effective practice in many subjects, including math (Gersten et al., 2009). Working with manipulatives helps students to verbalize the mathematics they are doing (Stein & Bovalino, 2001).

Emergent Bilinguals

It is extremely important to consider the needs of emergent bilingual students (Baumann, 2021). In designing acceleration programs we must consider how to meet the needs of these students. We must have ways to effectively assess their learning as opposed to their ability to speak the language. We need to have teaching, learning, and assessment opportunities that grow student achievement. To do this well, teachers must understand students' language acquisition levels. Knowledge of the students' language levels lets the teacher know how to effectively deliver the content and the ways to best scaffold demonstration. When we engage students and scaffold activity within their academic language levels, all students can actively participate in the lesson and show what they know and can do on grade level (Almeida, 2007; Echevarría & Graves, 2015).

It is important to consider the ways in which we are using "performance assessments, cooperative learning opportunities and the use of nonlinguistic representation (such as graphic organizers, dioramas, charts, and mental picture), as well as teacher observations in conjunction with rubrics" (Almeida, 2007, p. 153). We have to consider the ways we are assessing our students so that we get a more accurate, fuller picture of what they can do (Almeida, 2007; Silver & Kitchen, 2010). There is a great deal of research on how to effectively teach and reach emergent bilinguals (Almeida, 2007; Echevarría & Graves, 2015; Silva, 2019), as seen in Figure 5.15. As with all students, we need multiple opportunities to explore ideas and multiple ways to collect evidence of learning. In some instances, it may be best to have a test translated or have students answer in their native language to see if they understand the skills (Almeida, 2007).

PROFESSIONAL DEVELOPMENT

To do this type of work, districts and schools must commit to a long-term, scaffolded, high-quality professional learning program. Different teachers are at different places in knowing how to do this work. Research tells us that there are three types of teacher knowledge that we must be concerned with for high-quality instruction: subject matter knowledge, pedagogical content knowledge, and curricular knowledge (Shulman, 1986). The last type of knowledge includes understanding the progression of concepts from grade to grade. Teachers need to know all three of these knowledge domains and they must also understand the development of students if they are to create powerful learning experiences for them. There must be a strong commitment to differentiated professional learning so that all teachers—both novices and veterans—get what they need to teach our 21st-century students.

Figure 5.15. Strategies for Teaching Emergent Bilinguals

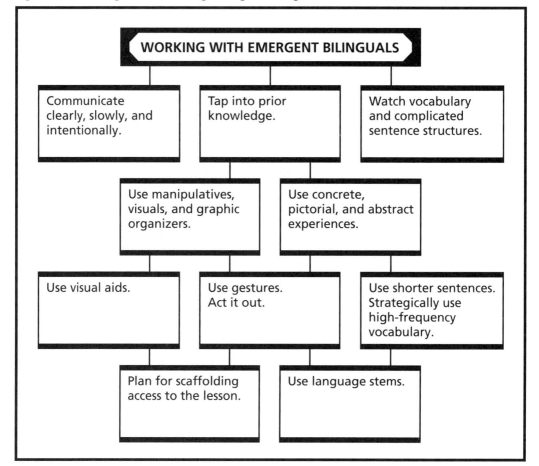

SUMMARY

Accelerating math instruction through targeted intervention requires that we fully engage students in the learning process. Teachers must make sure to hook the students at the beginning of the lesson, and must keep them engaged throughout with multisensory, academically rigorous, engaging lessons that connect to real life and personal experiences. Teachers should be sure to take students through a cycle of concrete, pictorial, and abstract experiences that lead them to fully grasp the concepts. Teachers should make sure that students are actively visualizing the math throughout the learning. Students should use a variety of manipulatives, diagrams, and graphic organizers that can help them access the mathematics. Teachers have to design experiences wherein students grow in confidence through successful encounters with mathematics and are motivated to learn more every day.

CHAPTER 6

Acceleration

A Primary Classroom Example

Many students struggle with multidigit addition and subtraction (Fuson & Briars, 1990; Fuson et al., 1997). Historically, in the United States students are taught "multidigit addition and subtraction as sequential procedures of adding and subtracting single-digit numbers and writing digits in certain locations" (Fuson et al., 1997). There have always been scholars who have advocated for a conceptual understanding of math rather than just a procedural understanding (Bay-Williams & Kling, 2019; Boaler, 2015; Brownell, 1956/1987). Over the past 10 years there has been a big push in many state standards to have students focus on using strategies based in place value, properties, and the relationship between addition and subtraction (NCTM, 2000).

It is important to make sure that students understand the basic facts of place value, properties, and the relationship between addition and subtraction so that they can carry these ideas through to multidigit addition and subtraction. In the accelerated lessons in this chapter we look at how that can be done. Fuson et al. (1997) advocate for a "'meaning maker' view of learning in which what a child 'sees' when looking at objects depends on the conceptual structures used by the child." These structures are supported "by having particular kinds of objects available, by kinds of use and discussion of such use by other children and adults in the classroom and by activities that help or direct the child in certain ways" (Fuson et al., 1997). Ebby et al. (2019) look at the important role manipulatives can play in the learning and internalizing of math strategies along the developmental progression. During math intervention, it is through the meaning making with each other and the use of various manipulatives and tools that student learning is scaffolded.

The ways in which we build, support, and extend understanding are vital to the learning process and happen over time (Fuson et al., 1997). Crespo et al. (2005) discuss the research and practice of explicitly teaching strategies to children, building on the work of Baroody (1985), Brownell (1956/1987), Fuson (2003), Rathmell (1978), and Steinberg (1985). Sometimes students invent their own strategies and at other times we explicitly teach them particular strategies (Bay-Williams & SanGiovanni, 2021). One of the major goals of the primary grades is to build mathematical proficiency, which means that students have conceptual understanding, procedural fluency, adaptive reasoning, strategic competence, and a productive disposition (NRC, 2001). Throughout the acceleration lessons the goal is that students understand and can explain the math they are doing, learn how to do the procedures with understanding, can think about the math in different ways, can reason about what they are doing, and have a good disposition.

JAMAL

Jamal is a 2nd-grade student. His class is working on 2-digit addition. However, he is struggling with 1-digit addition. His teacher is going to use acceleration to teach him on grade level. The teacher will need to scaffold what Jamal knows and use it to link to what he needs to know. Jamal will have to build up the skills of the prior knowledge and link as he goes along.

Goal: To accelerate the teaching of 2-digit addition.

The Standard: Single-digit addition within 20 and 2-digit addition within 100.

How: Teach Jamal the grade-level standard alongside filling in the gaps of what he doesn't know around this priority standard. At the same time, make connections between what he is currently studying in school and missing information.

Plan: Give Jamal a visual trajectory of what we will be working on (such as the one in Figure 6.1). Set out a 2-week intervention cycle of intensive learning sessions of 30 minutes each, 3 times a week. That will be a total of 90 minutes a week for 2 weeks. This will be the first round of acceleration lessons. The plan for these weeks appears in Figure 6.3.

LEARNING TRAJECTORY OF ADDITION

Children follow common developmental pathways as they learn math. Starting with basic facts and skills, they progress along a logical trajectory to more complex knowledge. One way to help students quickly gain ground on this path is to provide them with a visual map of the steps to come. Figure 6.1 shows a trajectory of early learning in addition that could be useful to Jamal.

Progression of Strategies for Addition

Crespo et al. (2005) said that there is "nothing basic about basic facts." To help children learn their basic math facts, it is important that teachers understand the progressions of strategies they can apply, but this is complicated by the fact that many of us did not learn our math facts in this way. Bay-Williams and SanGiovanni (2021) point out that it is important for students to understand, practice, and be able to select the correct strategies. We give students an opportunity to explore strategies, play around with strategies, and understand and develop strategies. We also teach some strategies.

Figure 6.1 shows a sequence of addition strategies and concepts that students should know by the end of 2nd grade (according to the most frequently applied standards, though standards used by a few states differ slightly). In kindergarten, the designated fluency is 5; in 1st grade, the designated fluency is 10. By 2nd grade, students are expected to achieve 2 fluencies: (1) addition

Figure 6.1. Addition Learning Trajectory, Kindergarten Through 2nd Grade

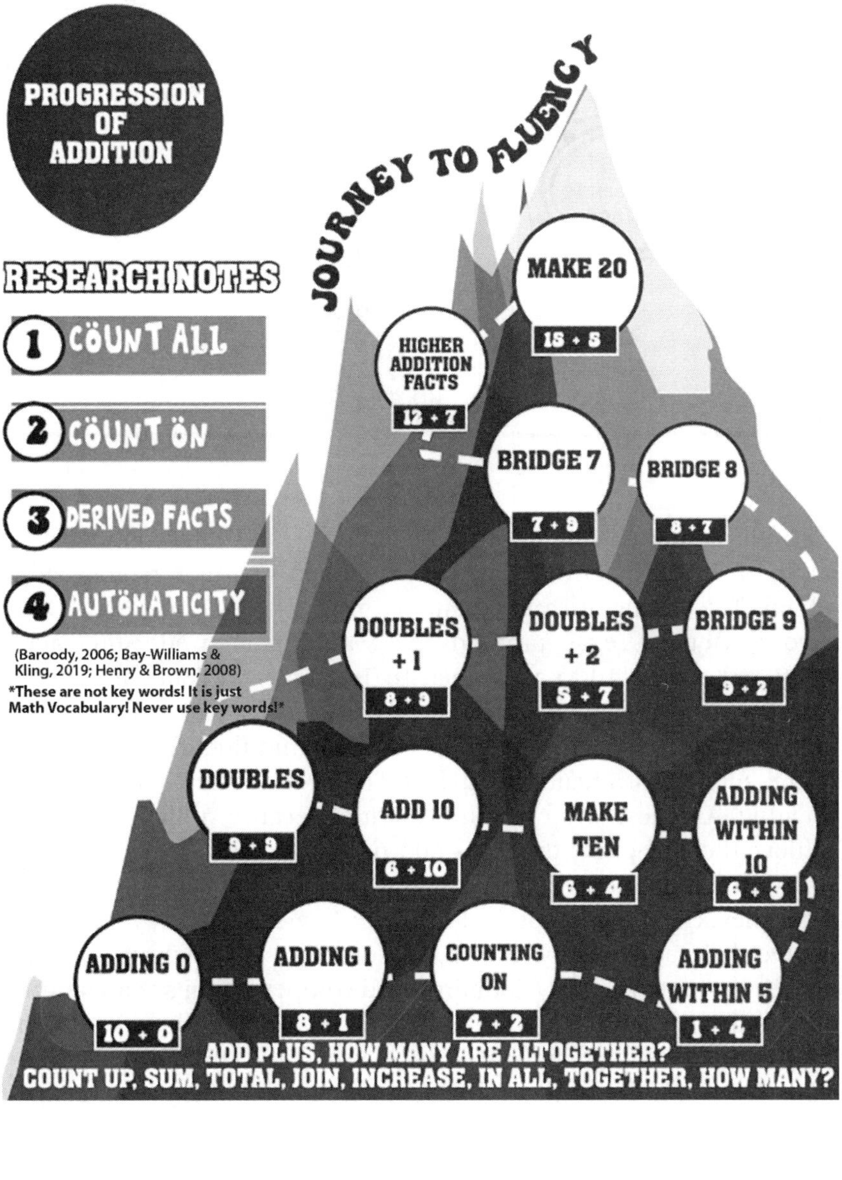

PROGRESSION OF ADDITION

JOURNEY TO FLUENCY

RESEARCH NOTES

1 COUNT ALL

2 COUNT ON

3 DERIVED FACTS

4 AUTOMATICITY

(Baroody, 2006; Bay-Williams & Kling, 2019; Henry & Brown, 2008)
These are not key words! It is just Math Vocabulary! Never use key words!

MAKE 20
15 + 5

HIGHER ADDITION FACTS
12 + 7

BRIDGE 7
7 + 9

BRIDGE 8
8 + 7

DOUBLES +1
8 + 9

DOUBLES +2
5 + 7

BRIDGE 9
9 + 2

DOUBLES
9 + 9

ADD 10
6 + 10

MAKE TEN
6 + 4

ADDING WITHIN 10
6 + 3

ADDING 0
10 + 0

ADDING 1
8 + 1

COUNTING ON
4 + 2

ADDING WITHIN 5
1 + 4

ADD PLUS, HOW MANY ARE ALTOGETHER?
COUNT UP, SUM, TOTAL, JOIN, INCREASE, IN ALL, TOGETHER, HOW MANY?

Figure 6.2. Strategies for Double-Digit Addition Within 100

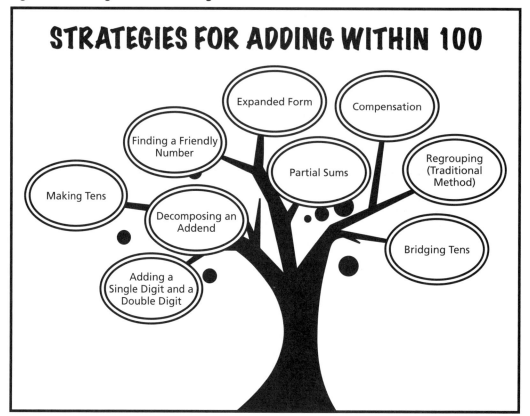

and subtraction within 20, and (2) addition and subtraction within 100. For addition, in the beginning, we want students to understand adding 1 and adding 0, counting on, and adding within 5. Next, by the end of 1st grade (or kindergarten, by Texas standards), we want them to understand adding within 10 and adding 10 to a number. In 1st grade, students are exposed to the 2nd-grade strategies but not expected to master them. By the end of 2nd grade, students are expected to thoroughly and fluently understand the rest of the addition strategies, including doubles, doubles + 1, doubles + 2, and bridging. All these strategies are essential because students will use them to achieve the 2nd-grade fluency—adding within 100.

As students move into 2nd grade, we want them to be able to connect what they know about basic addition facts with what they will need to do in double-digit addition within 100. Counting on, making tens (bridging), breaking numbers apart, doubling, and compensating are all addition strategies students should be able to transfer to work with larger numbers (see Figure 6.2). When students see 29 + 2, they could count on; when they see 30 + 30, they could double; and when they see 28 + 29, they could bridge through a ten. We lay a strong foundation and then build up.

Figure 6.3. Accelerated Math Lesson Checklist

Stage	Topic/Activity
Clear Learning Goal	Learning to add 2-digit numbers
Success Criteria	Students will know they can do it when they can • Model a problem • Explain their answer • Solve word problems • Compute sums • Create a problem to match an expression or equation
Engaging Launch	Looking at bridging 9 with manipulatives
Vocabulary	Addends, Sum, Strategies, Bridge 10
Review of Prior Content Skills Needed for This Concept	Bridging 10 with 1-digit numbers
Connection to Current Content	Bridging 10 with 2-digit numbers
Progress Monitoring	Workmat (including reflection), Anecdotals, Can student explain their work?
Feedback	Verbal and written
Student Check-In/Self-Reflection	On the reflection sheet

Acceleration Program Checklist

To ensure that we don't miss anything as we work with Jamal, we draw up a short checklist (see Figure 6.3) that covers the main stages and topics of the acceleration program: the learning goal, success criteria, launch, vocabulary, connections to prior knowledge, progress monitoring, feedback, and student self-monitoring. Explicitly planning for these elements allows us to make sure that we touch on each of them.

A WEEK OF SCAFFOLDING THE BRIDGING 10 STRATEGY: BIG IDEAS IN ADDITION

In this unit we will be building understanding of the concept of bridging 10. We want Jamal to be able to model and explain addition using place value, properties of operations, and the relationship between addition and subtraction. We will strategically look back to the 1st-grade standard of exploring strategies to add within 20. We will scaffold up to 2nd-grade fluency with these strategies and then bridge into the new concept of adding within 100. We will be working through a learning cycle of concrete, pictorial, and abstract lessons summarized in Figure 6.4.

Figure 6.4. Accelerated Learning Cycle: Addition

Teachers and students monitor progress through the lesson and adjust as necessary. Reflection is built into the workmat. Discussion is built into the lesson.

STEP 1 Assess specific knowledge, skills, and vocabulary for addition. Do an addition trace. (Start where students begin to have trouble.)

STEP 2 Go back through the targeted standard to teach the prior knowledge (content, strategies, skills). Trace addition back through 1st grade. Make connections explicit.

STEP 3 Hands-on, standard-based, academically rigorous tasks and activities to address prior knowledge. Use base-ten blocks, draw base-ten sketches. Write the equation.

STEP 4 Connect current grade-level standard to prior knowledge. Engage in rich tasks and activities. Make connections explicit. Provide scaffolds to access current content as needed. Use addition tables and charts.

STEP 5

Prior Knowledge/Schema. Figure 6.5 shows a trace for addition through 4th grade. We can look forward and back to instantly see the coherence across grade levels. It is important to make connections with not only the specific skill but also the vocabulary and the models.

Scaffolded Practice. Jamal will be given mini-posters, visual flashcards, and games to play at home to reinforce his learning. He can also use these tools to reference and practice in the math workstations. Jamal can also refer to the visual trajectory that was given to him at the beginning of the intervention (see Figure 6.1) to see the through line of learning.

Figure 6.5. Trace of Addition, Grades 1–4

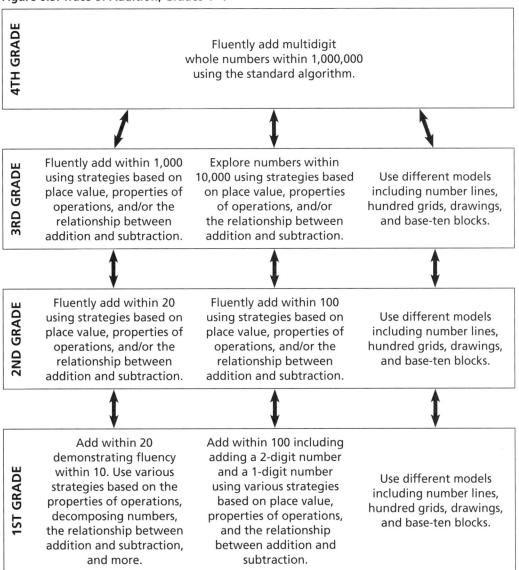

Note: These are standards from NGA and CCSSO (2010) and most current state standards.

Keeping Track. Throughout each lesson, the teacher will keep track of what is happening while working with students to get them to play an active role in their own learning. The teacher will make anecdotal notes about student affect—how they feel at the beginning of the lesson and how they feel at the end of the lesson. What do they do when they get stuck? What is their perseverance like, and how can that inform the teacher's moves toward building a growth mindset? Are students comprehending and using math vocabulary? At the end of the lesson, the teacher needs to collect evidence of learning. This can take place in a variety of ways. Along with the work shown on the workmat, exit slips can be great ways to collect evidence.

Assessment/Progress Monitoring. It is important to monitor progress throughout the lesson and across lessons. At the end of every week, the teacher should give a quick assessment to see if the intervention is working or not. Depending on the data, the teacher might need to continue the course, change course and reinforce more of what is being taught, or change the goals to something else.

TRACKING A ONE-WEEK ACCELERATION CYCLE

Jamal will start out tapping into the prior background knowledge needed to scaffold him into the current grade-level standard. In the first lesson he starts with adding within 20. The lesson sequence continues through the grade-level skill (see Figure 6.6). Sample forms that can be used with these lessons are included in this chapter.

In 2nd grade, students learn to get to the nearest 10 to make a problem easier to add, as one of many strategies. This strategy directly relates to the bridging 10 strategy that students learn when they are working on their basic addition facts. Jamal's teacher will start with this strategy and connect it to the new grade-level standard.

Figure 6.6. Sequence of Acceleration Lessons

Lesson 1	Review bridging 10 (Figure 6.8)
Lesson 2	Continue to practice bridging 10; the teacher can extend the conversation to working with 7 and 8 (Figure 6.10)
Lesson 3	Start bridging past 20 (Figure 6.12)
Lesson 4	Continue to use the bridging 10 strategy to add within 100 (Figure 6.14)
Lesson 5	Review the story of bridging 10 for adding within 100; students play games, work with visual flashcards, and review anchor charts about the strategy (Figure 6.15)
Lesson 6	Students take a written quiz and do a quick oral interview about using the bridging 10 strategy for adding within 100 (Figure 6.19)

Lesson 1

The teacher begins the lesson with asking students about strategies. What do they know from 1st grade? What do they remember? This gives the teacher an opening for talking about the strategy of bridging 10. The teacher starts with a poster that visually explains the strategy (see Figure 6.7). The goal of today is to bring up prior knowledge and begin to connect it with what students are going to be learning around the 2nd-grade standard (see Figure 6.8).

Content Questions:

1. What is bridging 10?
2. What are strategies we are learning?
3. What are models we are learning?

Cycle of Engagement:

1. *Concrete*—We listen to the problem. Act it out with the manipulatives.
2. *Pictorial*—We read the problem. Make a sketch and solve. Write the equation.
3. *Abstract*—We read and make sense of the problems. Model the problems in different ways.

Figure 6.7. Lesson 1. Poster: Bridging 10

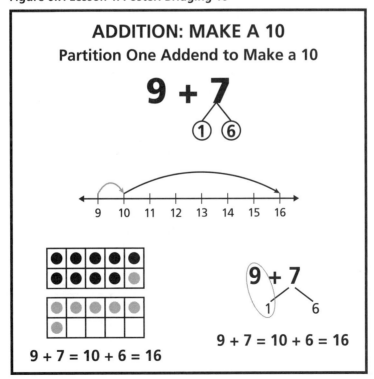

Figure 6.8. Lesson 1. Math Mat: Bridging 10

STORY: John had 9 marbles. He got 4 more for his birthday. How many does he have now?

MATH MAT: I am learning to bridge 10 to add.

9 + 4 = ?	What are strategies that I can use to add two single-digit numbers when there is a 9?

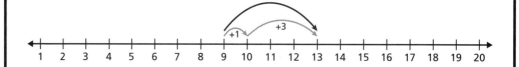

ACT IT OUT.

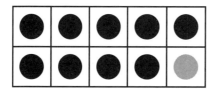 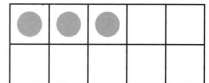

DRAW IT OUT.

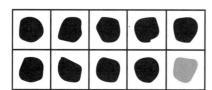 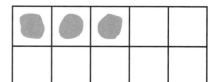

VOCABULARY	NOTES: REMEMBER TO
Add, addition, bridge 10, bridge up, strategy	

ADDEND ADDEND SUM	THIS REMINDS ME OF	REFLECTION
9 + 4 = ?		

Lesson 2

The teacher begins the lesson with asking students about strategies. They talk about what they have been studying. The goal of today is to bring in more models to look at the strategy (see Figures 6.9 and 6.10).

Content Questions:

1. What is bridging 10?
2. What are strategies we are learning?
3. What are models we are learning?

Cycle of Engagement:

- *Concrete*—We listen to the problem. Act it out with the manipulatives.
- *Pictorial*—We read the problem. Make a sketch and solve. Write the equation.
- *Abstract*—We read and make sense of the problems. Model them with ten frames and number lines and write the equations.

Figure 6.9. Lesson 2. Poster: Bridging 10

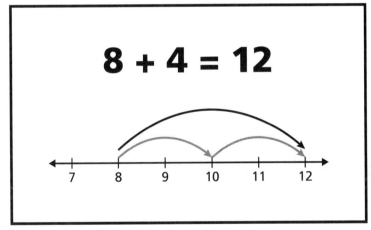

Figure 6.10. Lesson 2. Math Mat: Bridging 10

STORY: Maria had 9 rings. She got 3 more for her birthday. How many does she have now?

MATH MAT: I am learning to bridge 10 to add.

9 + 3 = ?	What are strategies that I can use to add two single-digit numbers when there is a 9?

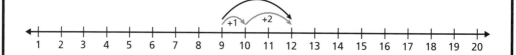

ACT IT OUT.

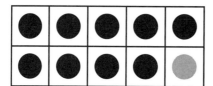 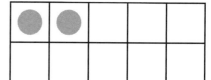

DRAW IT OUT.

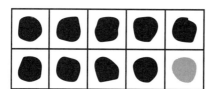 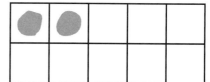

VOCABULARY	NOTES: REMEMBER TO
Add, addition, bridge 10, bridge up, strategy	

ADDEND ADDEND SUM	THIS REMINDS ME OF	REFLECTION
9 + 3 = ?		

80

Lesson 3

The teacher begins the lesson with asking students about strategies. They talk about what they have been studying over the past few days. The goal of today is to bring up prior knowledge and begin to make a direct connection with what students are going to be learning around the 2nd-grade standard (see Figures 6.11 and 6.12).

Content Questions:

1. What is bridging 10?
2. What are strategies we are learning?
3. What are models we are learning?

Cycle of Engagement:

- *Concrete*—We listen to the problem. Act it out with the manipulatives
- *Pictorial*—We read the problem. Make a sketch and solve. Write the equation.
- *Abstract*—We read and make sense of the problems. Model the problems in different ways.

Figure 6.11. Lesson 3. Poster: Bridging 10

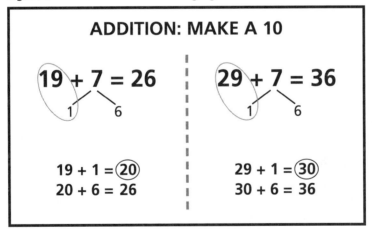

ADDITION: MAKE A 10

$$19 + 7 = 26$$

1   6

$$29 + 7 = 36$$

1   6

$19 + 1 = 20$
$20 + 6 = 26$

$29 + 1 = 30$
$30 + 6 = 36$

Figure 6.12. Lesson 3. Math Mat: Bridging 10

STORY: The bakery had 29 cupcakes. Then they made 8 more. How many did they have altogether?

MATH MAT: I am learning to bridge 10 to add.

29 + 8 = ?	What are strategies that I can use to add a double-digit number and a single-digit number when there is a 7, 8, or 9?

1 2 3 4 5 6 7 8 9 10 11 12 13 14 15 16 17 18 19 20 21 22 23 24 25 26 27 28 29 30 31 32 33 34 35 36 37 38 39 40

ACT IT OUT.

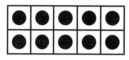 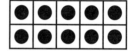

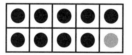 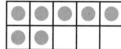

DRAW IT OUT.

Students would act out the problem on a hundreds grid.

1	2	3	4	5	6	7	8	9	10
11	12	13	14	15	16	17	18	19	20
21	22	23	24	25	26	27	28	29	30
31	32	33	34	35	36	37	38	39	40
41	42	43	44	45	46	47	48	49	50
51	52	53	54	55	56	57	58	59	60
61	62	63	64	65	66	67	68	69	70
71	72	73	74	75	76	77	78	79	80
81	82	83	84	85	86	87	88	89	90
91	92	93	94	95	96	97	98	99	100

VOCABULARY	NOTES: REMEMBER TO
Add, addition, bridge 10, bridge up, strategy	

ADDEND ADDEND SUM	THIS REMINDS ME OF	REFLECTION
29 + 8 = ?		

Lesson 4

The teacher continues with this cycle of learning through three more lessons focusing on bridging 10, using visual scaffolds, games, and bridging 10 visual flashcards. Students are given a quiz on bridging 10 (see Figure 6.19). It is preferable to give the students a few days to digest the learning from Lesson 3 before giving them a quiz.

In Lesson 4, the teacher is accelerating up to the 2nd-grade standard of adding within 100, focusing on bridging 10 and using different models. The goal is to make direct connections with what the students have been practicing (see Figures 6.13 and 6.14).

Content Questions:

- What is bridging 10?
- What are strategies we are learning?
- What are models we are learning?

Cycle of Engagement:

- *Concrete*—We listen to the problem. Act it out with the manipulatives (place-value blocks).
- *Pictorial*—We read the problem. Make a sketch and solve. Write the equation.
- *Abstract*—We read and make sense of the problems. Model them. Write equations. Discuss.

Figure 6.13. Lesson 4. Poster: Bridging 10

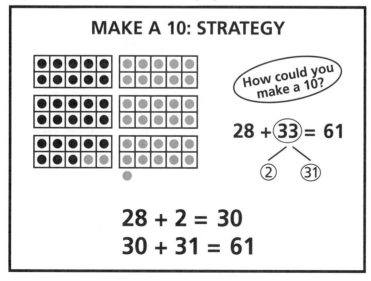

Figure 6.14. Lesson 4. Math Mat: Bridging 10

STORY: Hong had $39. He got $15 more more.
How much money does he have now?

MATH MAT: I am learning to bridge 10 to add.

39 + 15 = ?	What are strategies that I can use to add two double-digit numbers when there is a 7, 8, or 9?

1 2 3 4   27 28 29 30 31 32 33 34 35 36 37 38 39 40 41 42 43 44 45 46 47 48 49 50 51 52 53 54 55 56 57 58 59 60

ACT IT OUT.

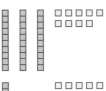

Students would make a ten out of the ones and would then have 5 tens and 4 ones.

DRAW IT OUT.

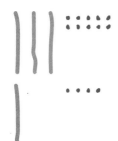

1	2	3	4	5	6	7	8	9	10
11	12	13	14	15	16	17	18	19	20
21	22	23	24	25	26	27	28	29	30
31	32	33	34	35	36	37	38	39	40
41	42	43	44	45	46	47	48	49	50
51	52	53	54	55	56	57	58	59	60
61	62	63	64	65	66	67	68	69	70
71	72	73	74	75	76	77	78	79	80
81	82	83	84	85	86	87	88	89	90
91	92	93	94	95	96	97	98	99	100

Students would act out the problem on a hundreds grid.

VOCABULARY
Add, addition, bridge 10, bridge up, strategy

NOTES: REMEMBER TO

ADDEND ADDEND SUM	THIS REMINDS ME OF	REFLECTION
39 + 15 = ?		

Lessons 5 and 6

These lessons are geared for practice and review. Students play with flashcards, dominos, and various board games to reinforce the concepts and skills they have been working on (see Figures 6.15 and 6.16). Notice that some of the work is scaffolded (e.g., the bridging 10 flashcards). Other practice is not scaffolded but is still engaging (e.g., the abstract practice tic-tac-toe game).

Figure 6.15. Bridging 10 Flashcards

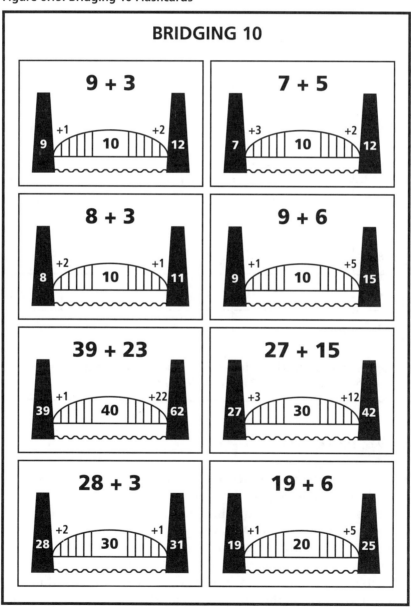

Figure 6.16. Bridging 10 Tic-Tac-Toe Game

ADDITION TIC-TAC-TOE

Board A

Bridging 10

9+5=☐	9+2=☐	9+8=☐
9+3=☐	9+4=☐	9+7=☐
2+9=☐	9+9=☐	9+6=☐

2+9=☐	7+9=☐	8+9=☐
6+9=☐	3+9=☐	9+9=☐
5+9=☐	9+5=☐	4+9=☐

9+4=☐	9+5=☐	9+7=☐
9+2=☐	4+9=☐	9+8=☐
9+6=☐	9+3=☐	9+9=☐

9+9=☐	7+9=☐	3+9=☐
9+8=☐	8+9=☐	9+5=☐
2+9=☐	6+9=☐	4+9=☐

9+9=☐	9+6=☐	9+5=☐
9+8=☐	9+3=☐	8+9=☐
9+4=☐	9+7=☐	9+2=☐

3+9=☐	5+9=☐	6+9=☐
7+9=☐	9+3=☐	9+8=☐
8+9=☐	9+9=☐	9+2=☐

9+3=☐	9+8=☐	3+9=☐
9+7=☐	9+2=☐	9+9=☐
9+5=☐	9+4=☐	9+6=☐

8+9=☐	2+9=☐	3+9=☐
5+9=☐	7+9=☐	4+9=☐
6+9=☐	9+9=☐	9+3=☐

9+6=☐	9+2=☐	9+3=☐
6+9=☐	9+7=☐	9+4=☐
9+9=☐	9+8=☐	9+5=☐

Instructions: Play rock-paper-scissors to see who starts. Then take turns answering a problem on the mat. Whoever gets 3 in a row first wins.

Overview of the Lessons

This series of lessons illustrates how we can connect prior knowledge directly to the new knowledge being taught. We form a direct trace between what students already understand, what they need to know, and what they should be able to do with their new learning. It is imperative that we teach all our students on grade level. The only way to do that is to give those who need help the necessary scaffolds to access the content. Math talk is part of the bridge to understanding. Along the way, students must continuously explain their thinking—what they are doing and why they are doing it. They need to talk about what they understand and where they are still confused. We must set up lessons that make explicit connections between the old and the new knowledge.

LESSON PLANNING

Now that we've walked through what content will be covered in each of the six lessons, as well as the strategies and tools we used to help Jamal, we can consider other aspects of lesson planning.

There are many different ways to plan for acceleration. A template provides a convenient starting point, and it can be more or less complex, depending on the needs and inclinations of the teacher. The important thing is that you *do* plan, in order to conduct the most effective interventions.

Two sample lesson planning templates are provided here. Additional examples appear in Chapters 7 and 8: Figures 7.14, 7.15, 8.18, and 8.19.

The planning template shown in Figure 6.17 covers the major stages of an intervention lesson: launch, main activity, guided and independent practice activities, assessment, and wrap-up. In addition, space is included for observations. A valuable feature of this template is columns that accommodate entries for individual student interventions and special considerations.

Figure 6.18 shows a lesson observation template. Included are spaces for observations of several students during major phases of the intervention, as well as space for noticings that might not fit into any specific category.

PROGRESS MONITORING

Progress monitoring takes place throughout the intervention cycle. The teacher should note everything that happens: the words, the student's affect, the student's ability to tap into prior knowledge, and the student's work. The teacher can collect and keep the intervention lesson mats as evidence of the learning journey. Formal progress monitoring should take place after the third lesson and after the final lesson in the intervention round. Figures 6.19 and 6.20 show examples of evaluation workmats for these two monitoring periods.

Throughout the week, students participate in various forms of assessment to check conceptual knowledge, procedural knowledge, reasoning, disposition, and strategic competence. The workmats in Figures 6.19 and 6.20 show examples of monitoring disposition with a quick emoji check-in. You can also do mini-interviews where you ask students to explain a strategy to check not only for procedural knowledge but also for conceptual knowledge. Figure 6.21 shows exit slips that check for procedural knowledge, strategic competence, and student reasoning.

Figure 6.17. Lesson Planning

MATH INTERVENTION LESSON PLAN				
Interventionist: Date:		Lesson: Focus:		
Prior Knowledge:		Manipulatives/Scaffolds:		
	Students			
"I Am Learning"/"I Can"				
Launch				
Main Activity				
Guided Practice				
Independent Practice				
Assessment				
Wrap-Up				
Observations				

Figure 6.18. Lesson Observation Template

MATH INTERVENTION LESSON OBSERVATIONS					
Interventionist: Date:		Lesson: Focus:			
Prior Knowledge: Goal: Success Criteria:		Manipulatives/Scaffolds:			
	Student 1	Student 2	Student 3	Student 4	Student 5
Observations During Energizers/Routines					
Observations During Demo/Modeling					
Observations During Exploration					
Observations During Independent Practice					
Other Noticings					

Figure 6.19. Progress Monitoring: End of the First Round of Lessons

BRIDGING 10

Solve this problem by sketching on the ten-frame.

7 + 4

Solve this problem. Model your thinking.

18 + 5

Solve this problem using the number line.

9 + 6

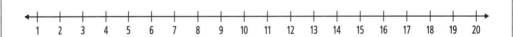

Solve this problem.

29 + 15

1	2	3	4	5	6	7	8	9	10
11	12	13	14	15	16	17	18	19	20
21	22	23	24	25	26	27	28	29	30
31	32	33	34	35	36	37	38	39	40
41	42	43	44	45	46	47	48	49	50

How are you doing with this concept? Circle the face that shows how you feel.

Figure 6.20. Summative Evaluation: End of the Intervention Round

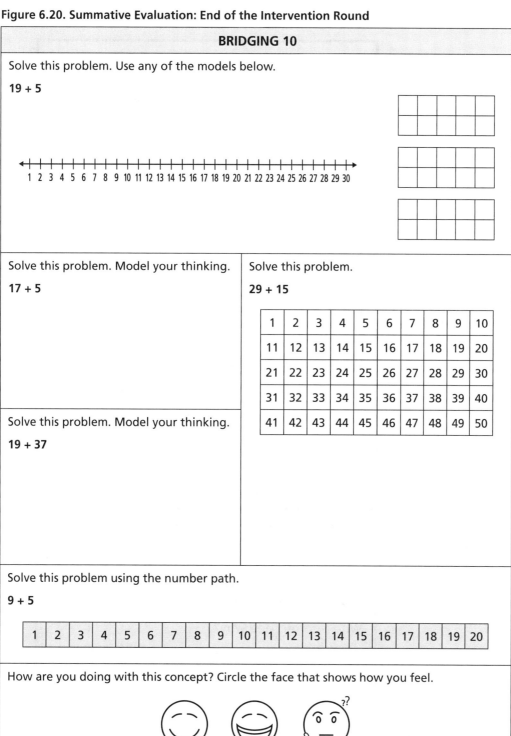

BRIDGING 10

Solve this problem. Use any of the models below.

19 + 5

Solve this problem. Model your thinking.

17 + 5

Solve this problem. Model your thinking.

19 + 37

Solve this problem.

29 + 15

1	2	3	4	5	6	7	8	9	10
11	12	13	14	15	16	17	18	19	20
21	22	23	24	25	26	27	28	29	30
31	32	33	34	35	36	37	38	39	40
41	42	43	44	45	46	47	48	49	50

Solve this problem using the number path.

9 + 5

1	2	3	4	5	6	7	8	9	10	11	12	13	14	15	16	17	18	19	20

How are you doing with this concept? Circle the face that shows how you feel.

Figure 6.21. Exit Slips

PROCEDURAL KNOWLEDGE

Name: _____   Date: _____

EXIT SLIP: Models and Equations

Solve 8 + 4. Model your thinking.

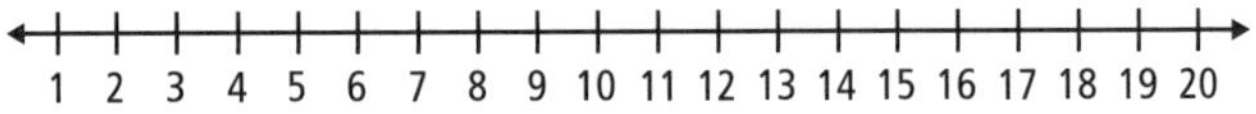

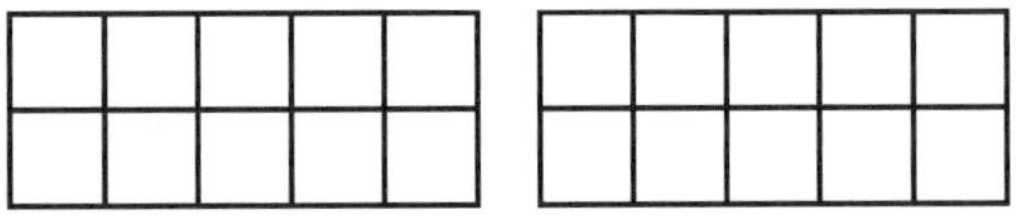

STRATEGIC COMPETENCE

Name: _____   Date: _____

EXIT SLIP

What are two ways to solve this problem? **28 +17**

Way 1	Way 2

STUDENT REASONING

Name: _____   Date: _____

EXIT SLIP

Luke said that 29 + 12 is 31. Lara said that it is 41.

Who is correct and why?

REFLECTING ON THE ACCELERATION CYCLE

It is important to reflect on the acceleration cycle. You have to figure out what went well, what needs to be changed, and what could be done differently. The reflection prompts in Figure 6.22 can be helpful in this reflection and planning.

Figure 6.22. Evaluating Acceleration: Reflection Activity

Reflection Question	Response
What lessons did you do during this acceleration cycle?	*Reviewed bridging 10 with 1-digit numbers and then with 2-digit numbers.*
Why did you choose those lessons?	*Because they followed a targeted trajectory of learning.*
How did you engage the students throughout the lessons?	*We did concrete, pictorial, and abstract activities. We monitored progress along the way. We used base-ten blocks, drawings, ten frames, number grids, and number lines.*
How did you check for understanding throughout the lesson?	*Asked questions. Had students explain their work. Did understanding check-ins with response cards.*
What kind of guided practice did you give the students?	*We did a problem together. They did a problem with a partner. They did a problem on their own.*
How do you know they learned the concepts?	*I know they were practicing the concepts. I know that they are now more familiar with the concepts. They are learning the concepts. I can tell this by their level of work and their conversations.*
What is the evidence of learning?	*The workmat has evidence that they can use the designated models. The discussion also provides evidence of understanding. The reflection gives some insight as well.*
How did you incorporate academic language throughout the lesson?	*The language is previewed before the lesson, used throughout the lesson (on the workmat as well), and reviewed at the end of the lesson.*
What went really well?	*The students could picture what we were doing. Using the manipulatives and teaching this through the telling of stories helped students to understand the concept.*
Would you do anything differently next time? Why or why not?	*I wish I had more days.*
Do you have anything else to add?	*We have to continue having students engage in meaningful practice at home.*

SUPPORTING THE ACCELERATION CYCLE

Throughout this chapter, you have seen numerous methods of providing scaffolding and practice for students: flashcards, strategy posters, board games, addition charts, and vocabulary support. The posters can be used during the lessons, hung up in the classroom, sent home, and kept in student math thinking notebooks as a reminder of what the strategy is about. Addition charts, wheels, and tables (see Figure 6.23) are another way for students to check their work. Charts and wheels are not as popular as tables, but they are easier to read and find answers in when students are playing games and need to check their work.

"I Can" Statements and Success Criteria

"I Can" statements are also helpful reminders to students of the lesson focus, while also encouraging them to have a positive math mindset. "I Can" posters like the ones in Figure 6.24 should be hung up in the room and discussed in small groups; also, students can have their own copies to keep in their math thinking notebooks. A poster highlighting success criteria is shown in Figure 6.25.

Differentiated Board Games

Students love board games. They are great standards-based, engaging, and rich sources to practice facts. The goal is to get students to have opportunities to practice. It is important to differentiate board games to give all students an opportunity to practice on grade level (see Figure 6.26). For example, students can play a game that has a number line or a bridging 10 frame chart to reference. Another example is a board game where students spin and state the strategy. For example, during a game, students might say:

- 9 + 1—That's a make 10 fact.
- 9 + 3—I'll count on and get 10, 11, 12.
- 9 + 5—I'll bridge 10. That is, 1 more to 10 and then 4 more makes 14.

Visual and Traditional Flashcards

There are many types of fabulous flashcards that can scaffold understanding (see Figure 6.27 for some examples). It is important to have flashcards that scaffold understanding through visual supports. Eventually students will work with traditional flashcards for basic recall, after they have a strong understanding of concepts.

Figure 6.23. Addition Table and Addition Charts

ADDITION TABLE										
+	**1**	**2**	**3**	**4**	**5**	**6**	**7**	**8**	**9**	**10**
1	2	3	4	5	6	7	8	9	10	11
2	3	4	5	6	7	8	9	10	11	12
3	4	5	6	7	8	9	10	11	12	13
4	5	6	7	8	9	10	11	12	13	14
5	6	7	8	9	10	11	12	13	14	15
6	7	8	9	10	11	12	13	14	15	16
7	8	9	10	11	12	13	14	15	16	17
8	9	10	11	12	13	14	15	16	17	18
9	10	11	12	13	14	15	16	17	18	19
10	11	12	13	14	15	16	17	18	19	20

ADDITION CHARTS

1 + 0 = 1	2 + 0 = 2	3 + 0 = 3	6 + 0 = 6	7 + 0 = 7	8 + 0 = 8
1 + 1 = 2	2 + 1 = 3	3 + 1 = 4	6 + 1 = 7	7 + 1 = 8	8 + 1 = 9
1 + 2 = 3	2 + 2 = 4	3 + 2 = 5	6 + 2 = 8	7 + 2 = 9	8 + 2 = 10
1 + 3 = 4	2 + 3 = 5	3 + 3 = 6	6 + 3 = 9	7 + 3 = 10	8 + 3 = 11
1 + 4 = 5	2 + 4 = 6	3 + 4 = 7	6 + 4 = 10	7 + 4 = 11	8 + 4 = 12
1 + 5 = 6	2 + 5 = 7	3 + 5 = 8	6 + 5 = 11	7 + 5 = 12	8 + 5 = 13
1 + 6 = 7	2 + 6 = 8	3 + 6 = 9	6 + 6 = 12	7 + 6 = 13	8 + 6 = 14
1 + 7 = 8	2 + 7 = 9	3 + 7 = 10	6 + 7 = 13	7 + 7 = 14	8 + 7 = 15
1 + 8 = 9	2 + 8 = 10	3 + 8 = 11	6 + 8 = 14	7 + 8 = 15	8 + 8 = 16
1 + 9 = 10	2 + 9 = 11	3 + 9 = 12	6 + 9 = 15	7 + 9 = 16	8 + 9 = 17
1 + 10 = 11	2 + 10 = 12	3 + 10 = 13	6 + 10 = 16	7 + 10 = 17	8 + 10 = 18

4 + 0 = 4	5 + 0 = 5	9 + 0 = 9	10 + 0 = 10
4 + 1 = 5	5 + 1 = 6	9 + 1 = 10	10 + 1 = 11
4 + 2 = 6	5 + 2 = 7	9 + 2 = 11	10 + 2 = 12
4 + 3 = 7	5 + 3 = 8	9 + 3 = 12	10 + 3 = 13
4 + 4 = 8	5 + 4 = 9	9 + 4 = 13	10 + 4 = 14
4 + 5 = 9	5 + 5 = 10	9 + 5 = 14	10 + 5 = 15
4 + 6 = 10	5 + 6 = 11	9 + 6 = 15	10 + 6 = 16
4 + 7 = 11	5 + 7 = 12	9 + 7 = 16	10 + 7 = 17
4 + 8 = 12	5 + 8 = 13	9 + 8 = 17	10 + 8 = 18
4 + 9 = 13	5 + 9 = 14	9 + 9 = 18	10 + 9 = 19
4 + 10 = 14	5 + 10 = 15	9 + 10 = 19	10 + 10 = 20

Figure 6.24. "I Can" Posters

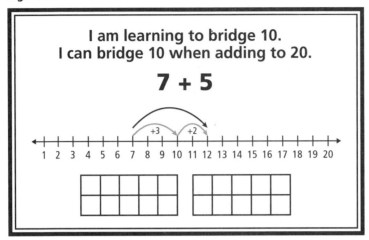

I am learning to bridge 10.
I can bridge 10 when adding to 20.

7 + 5

I am learning to bridge 10. I can bridge 10 when adding to 100.

38 + 24

1	2	3	4	5	6	7	8	9	10
11	12	13	14	15	16	17	18	19	20
21	22	23	24	25	26	27	28	29	30
31	32	33	34	35	36	37	38	39	40
41	42	43	44	45	46	47	48	49	50
51	52	53	54	55	56	57	58	59	60
61	62	63	64	65	66	67	68	69	70
71	72	73	74	75	76	77	78	79	80
81	82	83	84	85	86	87	88	89	90
91	92	93	94	95	96	97	98	99	100

Figure 6.25. Success Criteria

I CAN BRIDGE 10

I will know it when I can mentally recognize the bridge 10 strategy.

Facts where there is a 7, 8, or 9.

Figure 6.26. Game Boards

97

Figure 6.27. Visual and Traditional Flashcards

VISUAL FLASHCARD WITH A WRITTEN HINT

These are great cards to visually scaffold the concept of bridging 10. Students who need that scaffold can benefit from using these cards in the beginning and then eventually phasing them out.

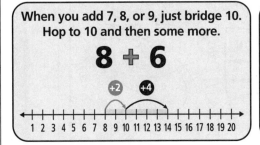

TRADITIONAL FLASHCARD

In this traditional game of **largest sum**, students will each pull a card and state the sum. Reinforce the vocabulary by having them say, "My sum is . . . ." Whoever has the largest sum wins both cards. Whoever has the most cards at the end of the game is the winner.

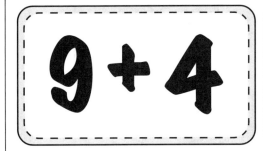

SUMMARY

In these examples of 2nd-grade lessons in addition, we see the teacher building on knowledge from 1st grade that is revisited in 2nd grade. In 2nd grade, the bridging 10 strategy becomes part of what students are supposed to know and be able to do in order to add fluently within 20. In addition, they are expected to then build on that skill and add fluently within 100. This takes a great deal of practice with the building 10 concept. Students should be given time to really understand this strategy, because they will continue to use it with multidigit numbers. Building 10 is just one of many strategies that students will learn as part of their designated grade-level fluency. It is important that students get to learn, work with, and practice various strategies throughout the year.

CHAPTER 7

Acceleration

An Upper Elementary Case Study

In this chapter we look at division, an operation that troubles many students. This is connected to the fact that many of them have not mastered their multiplication tables. Therefore, they can't use division's inverse operation because they don't know it yet. This is another reason why it is important to work on fluency for 10 minutes a day during acceleration interventions (IES, 2009).

Division is the most difficult arithmetic operation to learn for all students (Fauzan et al., 2020; Götze, 2018; Lajoie & Maheux, 2013). Researchers have found that students apply various division strategies on a regular basis in all grades, including use of factual knowledge and recourse to multiplication and to repeated addition (Downton, 2008; Robinson et al., 2006). Even though students can sometimes solve problems, often they still don't know what they are doing and can't explain it (Bryant, 1997; Götze, 2018). Students who struggle with math overall have an even more difficult time with division (Robinson & LeFevre, 2012).

Cawley et al. (2001) notes that the introduction of division is the "cut-off" point for many children. Feldman (2012) points out that without an understanding of division, students have real problems with the rest of arithmetic. The focus needs to be on building a conceptual understanding of division (Downton, 2008; Moser Optiz, 2013, as cited in Götze, 2018). There must be an emphasis on the relationship between multiplication and division to develop understanding of division (Downton, 2008; Moser Optiz, 2013, as cited in Götze, 2018; Robinson & LeFevre, 2012).

Language also plays a major role in the teaching and learning of division (Anghileri, 1995; Downton, 2008). This situation becomes even more exacerbated for learners who are struggling with math (Cawley et al., 2001). Hammond and Gibbons (2005) argue that we need to strategically scaffold language. Downton (2008), too, notes that "placing emphasis on the relationship between multiplication and division and the language associated with both operations before any use of symbols or formal recording needs to be a priority" (p. 177). Scaffolding the language of division gives students a "language based understanding" (Götze, 2018). Feilke (2012, as cited in Götze, 2018) points out that phrases like "divided into," "divided by," or ". . .

times . . . makes" are used often but are meaningless. "Using phrases like '20 divided into two groups of ten each', 'four fives in 20' or when describing a specific problem 'a divisor fits in a number without remainder' shows the thinking practice of the children—a thinking practice that is deeply connected to the 'language of schooling'" (Feilke, 2012, as cited in Götze, 2018).

To build conceptual understanding, teachers need to be familiar with and understand how to use learning trajectories to inform their instructional journeys (Daro et al., 2011). Students can reason about division when they are given real-life contexts. Fauzan et al. (2020) argue that it is important for teachers to watch what students are doing and ask them why they are doing that, and then help them to reason about the math. Lajoie and Maheux (2013) point out that often teachers have trouble teaching the concept of division, especially division with remainders, and students have great difficulty understanding it. Downton (2008) notes that students can solve complex division problems if they are encouraged to reason about the problems and use multiplication. They need a variety of real-life experiences working with division. In acceleration cycles we must slowly build a conceptual understanding and scaffold through the different types of division, including division with remainders.

LUCY

Lucy is a 4th-grade student. Her class is working on division of 2-, 3-, and 4-digit numbers by 1-digit numbers. However, Lucy is struggling with basic division. After giving her a division running record to determine where her errors were occurring and where she was stuck, the teacher determined that she needed to start at the beginning of division. At first, Lucy didn't even show understanding of basic ideas of division, including dividing 0 by a number, dividing by 1, or dividing a number by itself. Research has found that these are typically the most difficult problems for students.

Goal: To accelerate the teaching of division of 2-, 3-, and 4-digit numbers by 1-digit numbers.

The Standard: Finding quotients of 2-, 3-, and 4-digit numbers when dividing by a 1-digit number.

How: Teach Lucy the grade-level standard alongside filling in the gaps of what she doesn't know around this priority standard. At the same time, make connections between what she is currently studying in school and the targeted prior standards so that she can learn the grade-level content.

Plan: Give Lucy a visual trajectory of what we will be working on (such as the one in Figure 7.1 or in Figure 7.2). Set out a 2-week intervention cycle of intensive learning sessions of 30 minutes each, 3 times a week. That will be a total of 90 minutes a week for 2 weeks. This will be the first round of acceleration lessons. The plan for these weeks appears in Figure 7.3.

LEARNING TRAJECTORY OF DIVISION

In the trajectory shown in Figure 7.1 and the overview of division shown in Figure 7.2, students can see the different things they are learning in terms of division. They can see what they know and what they still need to learn.

Figure 7.1. Division Learning Trajectory, 4th Grade

Figure 7.2. Overview of Division Within 100

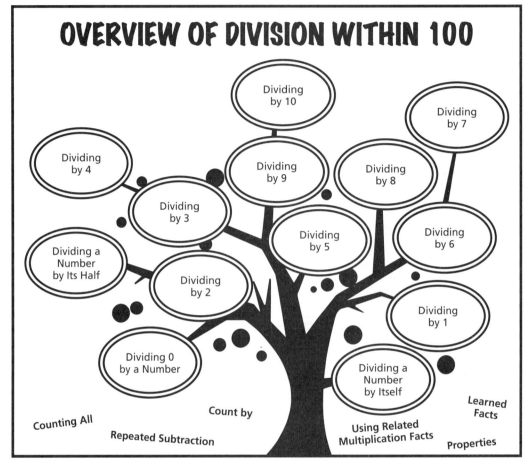

Progression of Learning in Division, Grades 3 and 4

At the beginning of learning division there are some foundational concepts that students need to grasp, such as dividing 0 by a number, dividing by 1, and dividing a number by itself. Research shows that students often have trouble with these concepts because they are difficult to grasp. Oftentimes, teachers don't spend much time building these concepts, because they appear easy; but really they are very difficult for many students.

In giving hundreds of math running records, I have seen this occur too often, even with students who know most of their facts. When they see 0 divided by a number, many students will say that can't be done. They often think that a number divided by itself is the number and a number divided by 1 is 1. When told a story about these expressions, most students can reason out the proper answers easily. This demonstrates that we must spend time contextualizing the operations so students can grasp the ideas.

Two other big conceptual ideas that students should understand are what happens when you divide a number by 2 and what happens when you divide a number by its half. For most of the other problems, a great strategy is to "think multiplication." But as many students have said to me, "I know I'm supposed to think multiplication, but I don't know my multiplication facts." We have to make sure students understand multiplication before we throw division at them. We should be trying to build that understanding and the connectedness of the operations as we are teaching them. That is why I love the fact family visual cards, because they help students see these relationships (see Figures 7.24C and 7.24D).

Acceleration Program Checklist

To ensure that we don't miss anything as we work with Lucy, we create a short checklist (see Figure 7.3) that includes the main stages and topics of the acceleration program: the learning goal, success criteria, launch, vocabulary, connections to prior knowledge, progress monitoring, feedback, and student self-monitoring. Explicitly planning for these elements allows us to make sure that we touch on each of them.

Figure 7.3. Accelerated Math Lesson Checklist

Stage	Topic/Activity
Clear Learning Goal	Learning to divide a 2-digit number by a 1-digit number with and without remainders.
Success Criteria	Students will know they can do it when they can • Model a problem • Explain their answer • Solve word problems • Compute quotients • Create a problem to match an expression or equation
Engaging Launch	Cupcake story
Vocabulary	Dividend, Divisor, Quotient, Factor, Multiply, Equation
Review of Prior Content Skills Needed for This Concept	Division within 100
Connection to Current Content	Division of 2-digit number by 1-digit number
Progress Monitoring	Workmat (including reflection), Anecdotals, Can student explain their work?
Feedback	Verbal and written
Student Check-In/Self-Reflection	On the reflection sheet

TWO WEEKS OF SCAFFOLDING DIVISION: BIG IDEAS IN DIVISION

In this unit we will work with Lucy to help her build understanding of the concept of division. She should be able to model and explain division with the area model, open arrays, and equations. We want her to work on developing fluency with the basic division facts and then be able to transfer those concepts, skills, and strategies to multidigit numbers. We will be working through a learning cycle of concrete, pictorial, and abstract lessons summarized in Figure 7.4.

Figure 7.4. Accelerated Learning Cycle: Division

Teachers and students monitor progress through the lesson and adjust as necessary. Reflection is built into the workmat. Discussion is built into the lesson.

Connect current grade-level standard to prior knowledge. Engage in rich tasks and activities. Make connections explicit. Provide scaffolds to access current content as needed. Use division charts, multiplication charts, multiplication and division tables.

Assess specific knowledge, skills, and vocabulary for division. Do a division trace.

Go back through the targeted standard to teach the prior knowledge (content, strategies, skills). Trace division standards to prior grades. Make connections explicit.

Hands-on, standard-based, academically rigorous tasks and activities to address prior knowledge. Work with various models and templates.

Figure 7.5. Trace of Division, Grades 3–6

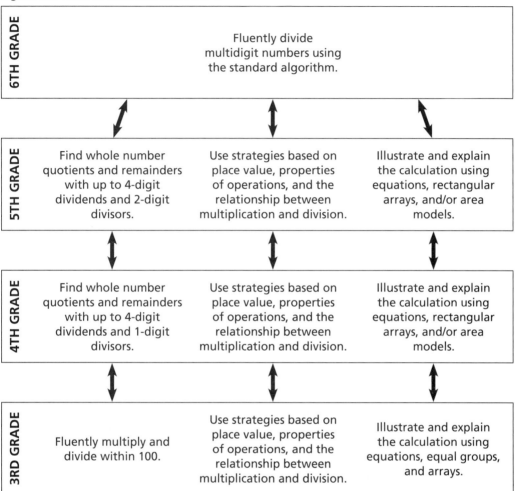

Note: These are standards from NGA and CCSSO (2010) and most current state standards.

Prior Knowledge/Schema. Figure 7.5 shows a trace for division in 3rd through 6th grades. We can look forward and back to instantly see the coherence across grade levels. It is important to make connections with not only the specific skill but also the vocabulary and the models.

Scaffolded Practice. Lucy will be given mini-posters, visual flashcards, and games to play at home to reinforce her learning (see Figures 7.20–7.24). She can use these tools to reference and practice in the math workstations as well. In addition, Lucy will be given multiplication and division mats. She can also refer to the visual trajectory that was given to her at the beginning of the intervention (see Figure 7.1) to see the through line of learning.

Keeping Track. Throughout each lesson, the teacher will keep track of what is happening while working with students to get them to play an active role in their own learning. The teacher will make anecdotal notes about student affect—how they feel at the beginning of the lesson and how they feel at the end of the lesson. What do they do when they get stuck? What is their perseverance like, and how can that inform the teacher's moves toward building a growth mindset? Are students comprehending and using math vocabulary? At the end of the lesson, the teacher will collect evidence of learning. This can take place in a variety of ways, including anecdotal comments, formative questions, student work artifacts, and teacher reflections.

Assessment/Progress Monitoring. It is important to monitor progress throughout the lesson and across lessons. At the end of every week, the teacher should give a quick assessment to see if the intervention is working or not. Depending on the data, the teacher might need to continue the course, change course and reinforce more of what is being taught, or change the goals to something else.

TRACKING A TWO-WEEK ACCELERATION CYCLE

Lucy will start out tapping into the prior background knowledge needed to scaffold her into the current grade-level standard. In Lesson 1 she is working on dividing within 100. This and the two following lessons are summarized in Figure 7.6, with more expansive versions illustrated in Figures 7.8, 7.10, and 7.12. Giving Lucy visual models like those in Figures 7.7, 7.9, and 7.11 and discussing them with her before she begins each lesson can help her activate prior knowledge and make connections to real life scenarios. Sample forms that can be used with these lessons are included in this chapter.

Figure 7.6. Sequence of Acceleration Lessons
The teacher might spend a few days on each lesson.

Lesson 1	Explore division within 100 (see Figure 7.8)
Lesson 2	Explore division with a remainder (see Figure 7.10)
Lesson 3	Explore division of a 2-digit number by a 1-digit number without a remainder and then with a remainder (see Figure 7.12)

Lesson 1

Figure 7.7A is a template for an anchor chart that can be developed in a review lesson about representing basic division facts. Students can discuss different ways to represent division, such as equal groups, arrays, area models, tape diagrams, and number bonds. They should also review the vocabulary associated with division. The anchor chart can be created with the students as a way of tapping into their prior knowledge and preparing them to move into the remainder of the lesson. It can also be used at the end of the lesson as a summation of what has been explored. Figure 7.7B shows a division poster used at the start of the lesson.

During the first sequence of lessons, we will work on partitive and quotative division. The first problems will explore partitive division, where students are looking for how many are in a group. These are the problems that teachers typically present in classrooms. In this lesson, students explore a story context about a bakery and act out the problems. Students will physically divide 12 cupcakes into 3 boxes and then as a small group we will discuss what this means.

In the next problem, we will work on quotative division, finding out the number of boxes needed. Research has shown that students have more difficulty with quotative problems than with partitive problems. Part of the reason is that we don't do as much of this type of division when we are first learning to divide. We should focus on both types of problems (see Figure 7.24A, which shows flashcards that illustrate the two types of problems).

Students are given a bakery story mat to act out different division problems at the concrete level. They get to explore dividing 0 by a number, dividing by 1, and dividing a number by itself; these often prove the three most difficult types of problems for students to conceptually understand. We also want students to understand what it means to divide a number by 2 and by its half. In most of the problems in this lesson, students are encouraged to think about multiplication as they work. First, we tell the story and solve one problem together. Then, students solve one problem with their partner. Then, they do one by themselves.

Figure 7.7A. Division Poster Template

MODELING DIVISION

EQUAL GROUPS	**ARRAYS**
AREA MODEL	**TAPE DIAGRAM**
OPEN ARRAY	**VOCABULARY**

Figure 7.7B. Lesson 1. Poster: Activating Prior Knowledge

MODELING DIVISION

$$20 \div 4 = 5$$

EQUAL GROUPS

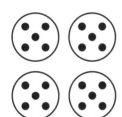

ARRAYS

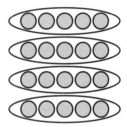

AREA MODEL

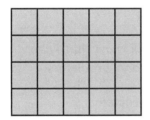

TAPE DIAGRAM

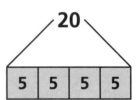

NUMBER BOND

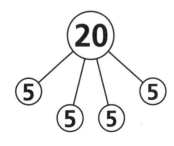

VOCABULARY

$$20 \div 4 = ?$$

Dividend   Divisor   Quotient

$$4 \times ? = 20$$

Factor   Missing   Product
          Factor

Students begin by working with a problem involving division by 3, and in each successive story mat they move on to explore dividing by 4 and 5 and other numbers (see Figures 7.8A–7.8C).

After some exploration, students look at representing the problem with other models, including a number bond, an area model, an array, and an equation. By filling out an anchor chart such as the division poster shown in Figure 7.8D, they also have a visual reminder of the vocabulary, a place to connect to past learning, and a reflection on the day's lesson. This type of reinforcement helps students to make connections, to think about what they are doing and how well they currently understand it, and to look at different representations that they will use throughout their journey of learning division. A recording sheet like the one shown in Figure 7.8E provides an additional place for students to practice with the material, reflect on the lesson, or perform a quick mini-assessment.

Figure 7.8A. Lesson 1. Story Mat: Dividing by 3

The bakery made 12 cupcakes and put them in 3 boxes. There were the same number of cupcakes in each box. How many cupcakes were in each?

THE
BAKERY

I can solve division word problems. I will know that I can do this when I can solve, tell, and model problems.

Pull a card and act out the problem.
Record your answer on the sheet.

Figure 7.8B. Lesson 1. Story Mat: Dividing by 4

The bakery made 16 cupcakes and put them in 4 boxes. There were the same number of cupcakes in each box. How many cupcakes were in each?

THE BAKERY

I can solve division word problems. I will know that I can do this when I can solve, tell, and model problems.

Pull a card and act out the problem.
Record your answer on the sheet.

Figure 7.8C. Lesson 1. Story Mat: Dividing by 5

The bakery made 20 cupcakes and put them in 5 boxes. There were the same number of cupcakes in each box. How many cupcakes were in each?

THE BAKERY

I can solve division word problems. I will know that I can do this when I can solve, tell, and model problems.

Pull a card and act out the problem.
Record your answer on the sheet.

Figure 7.8D. Lesson 1. Poster: Reinforcement

MODELING DIVISION

$$12 \div 3 = 4$$

EQUAL GROUPS 	**ARRAYS** 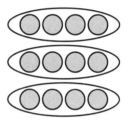
AREA MODEL 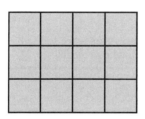	**TAPE DIAGRAM** 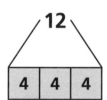
OPEN ARRAY	**VOCABULARY**

OPEN ARRAY

$$2 + 2$$

| 3 | 6 | 6 |

VOCABULARY

$$12 \div 3 = ?$$

Dividend   Divisor   Quotient

$$3 \times ? = 12$$

Factor   Missing   Product
Factor

Figure 7.8E. Lesson 1. Recording Sheet

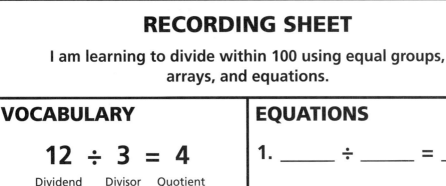

RECORDING SHEET

I am learning to divide within 100 using equal groups, arrays, and equations.

VOCABULARY

$$12 \div 3 = 4$$

Dividend   Divisor   Quotient

NOTES AND COMMENTS

EQUATIONS

1. _____ ÷ _____ = _____

2. _____ ÷ _____ = _____

3. _____ ÷ _____ = _____

REFLECTION

Lesson 2

Lesson 2 looks at division with remainders. The interpretation of remainders is always tricky for students. Problems with remainders are one of the types of word problems that 4th-graders often miss. Students are known for splitting people and buses into halves and fourths. It is important to contextualize remainder problems and have students act them out and discuss what is happening and how to interpret the remainder. We start by reviewing the models for division within 100 (see Figure 7.9). Next, we use these same models to explore remainders (see Figures 7.10A and 7.10B).

Figure 7.9. Lesson 2. Poster: Activating Prior Knowledge

MODELING DIVISION

$$27 \div 5 = 5\tfrac{2}{5}$$

EQUAL GROUPS

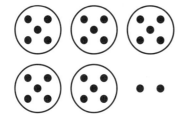

ARRAYS

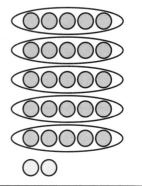

AREA MODEL

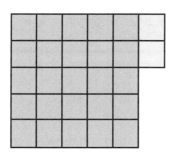

TAPE DIAGRAM

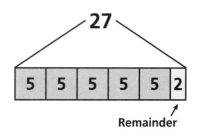

27

| 5 | 5 | 5 | 5 | 5 | 2 |

Remainder

OPEN ARRAY

4 + 1

| 5 | 20 | 5 | 2 |

Remainder

VOCABULARY

$$27 \div 5 = ?$$

Dividend   Divisor   Quotient

$$27 \div 5 = 5\tfrac{2}{5}$$

Dividend   Divisor   Quotient
with
remainder

Figure 7.10A. Lesson 2. Story Mat: Dividing by 3 With Remainders

The bakery made 14 cupcakes and put them in 3 boxes. There were the same number of cupcakes in each box. How many cupcakes were in each? Were there any left over?

THE BAKERY

I can solve division word problems. I will know that I can do this when I can solve, tell, and model problems.

Pull a card and act out the problem.
Record your answer on the sheet.

Figure 7.10B. Lesson 2. Story Mat: Dividing by 2 With Remainders

The bakery made 9 cupcakes and put them in 2 boxes. There were the same number of cupcakes in each box. How many cupcakes were in each? Were there any left over?

THE BAKERY

I can solve division word problems. I will know that I can do this when I can solve, tell, and model problems.

Pull a card and act out the problem.
Record your answer on the sheet.

Figure 7.10C. Lesson 2. Division With Bars on a Grid

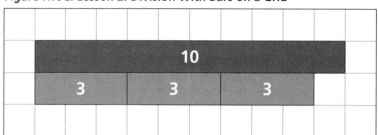

Cuisenaire™ rods are another great way to visually explore the concept of remainders. We ask the students "How many 3's can you take out of 10?" They can see that they can only take three 3's out of 10 and that there is a remainder of 1. We also teach students to write the answer as a fraction because the often-used R is actually mathematically incorrect (Dr. Hung His Wu, personal communication, February 27, 2020). Writing the answer as a fraction of 3⅓ and getting students to see that there are 3 wholes and ⅓ of another whole that can be taken out of 10 is an important understanding. We want students to be able to explain what the remainder means and that, depending on the context, it can be interpreted in different ways.

Another way to represent division is with bars on a grid (see Figure 7.10C). We do this work initially on centimeter grid paper so that students can practice showing it with a math sketch as well. We start with small numbers that they can make sense of.

Just as in Lesson 1, students continue to explore the number bond, the area model, the array, and equations. They also continue their emphasis on using the vocabulary to explain what is happening. They create visual reminders of the vocabulary, a place to connect to past learning, and a reflection on the day's lesson (see Figures 7.10D and 7.10E). We want students to be actively involved in explaining the math they are learning. Conversations should be embedded throughout the lesson.

Figure 7.10D. Lesson 2. Poster: Reinforcement

MODELING DIVISION

$$14 \div 3 = 4\tfrac{2}{3}$$

EQUAL GROUPS

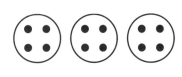

ARRAYS

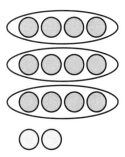

AREA MODEL

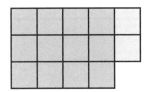

TAPE DIAGRAM

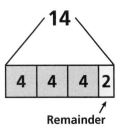

14

| 4 | 4 | 4 | 2 |

Remainder

OPEN ARRAY

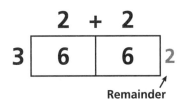

2 + 2

3 | 6 | 6 | 2

Remainder

VOCABULARY

$$14 \div 3 = ?$$

Dividend   Divisor   Quotient

$$14 \div 3 = 4\tfrac{2}{3}$$

Dividend   Divisor   Quotient with remainder

Figure 7.10E. Lesson 2. Recording Sheet

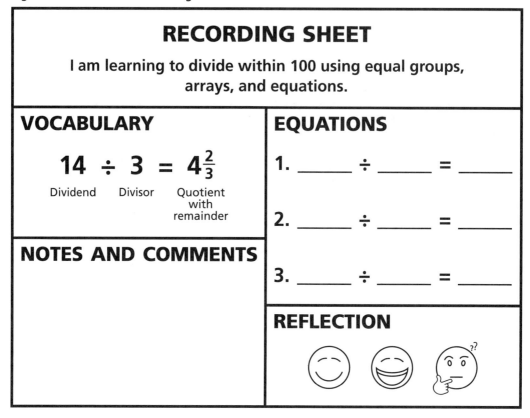

Lesson 3

After students have worked extensively with building their conceptual understanding of division and connecting that to the grade-level standard of working with remainders, they can use these same models to explore division with larger numbers. We will be working with more tools—such as place-value disks and place-value blocks—to encompass the scope of the numbers as we explore division of a multidigit number by a single-digit number.

In Figure 7.11 we explore the concept of dividing a multidigit number by a single-digit number. Through a series of activities, we explore using equal groups, arrays, the area model, tape diagrams/bar models, and equations. We start in the bakery again, but this time exploring 48 divided by 4, with base-ten blocks.

In the story mat in Figure 7.12A, we look at dividing 48 cupcakes into 4 boxes. We end up doing several problems where we are exploring equal groups. We also work with problems where we are looking for how many groups we have. In problems based on story mats such as the one shown in Figure 7.12B, remainders are introduced.

Figure 7.11. Lesson 3. Poster: Activating Prior Knowledge

MODELING DIVISION

$$48 \div 4 = 12$$

EQUAL GROUPS

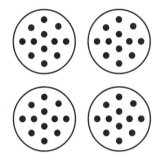

ARRAYS

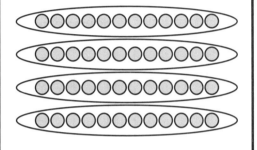

AREA MODEL

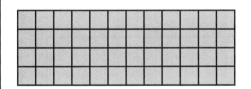

TAPE DIAGRAM

48

| 12 | 12 | 12 | 12 |

OPEN ARRAY

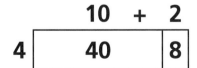

10 + 2

4 | 40 | 8 |

VOCABULARY

$$48 \div 4 = ?$$

Dividend   Divisor   Quotient

$$4 \times ? = 48$$

Factor   Missing Factor   Product

Figure 7.12A. Lesson 3. Story Mat: Dividing by a Single-Digit Number

The bakery made 48 cupcakes and put them in 4 boxes. There were the same number of cupcakes in each box. How many cupcakes were in each?

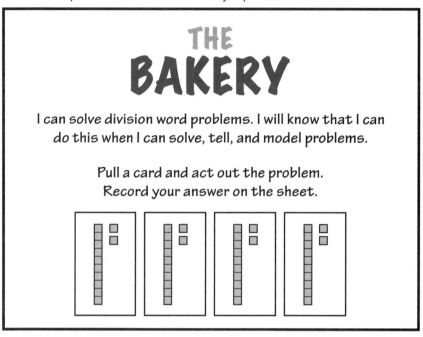

Figure 7.12B. Lesson 3. Story Mat: Dividing by a Single-Digit Number With Remainders

The bakery made 52 cupcakes and had 5 boxes to put them in. There were the same number of cupcakes in each box. The baker gave away the leftovers. How many cupcakes were in each box? How many were left over?

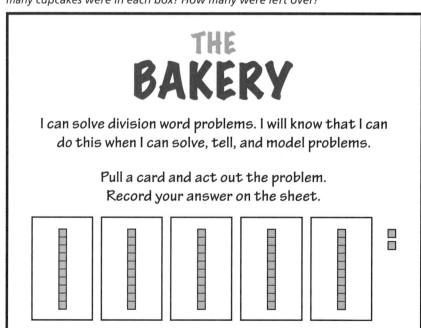

Figure 7.12C. Lesson 3. Division With the Area Model: 22 ÷ 2 = ?

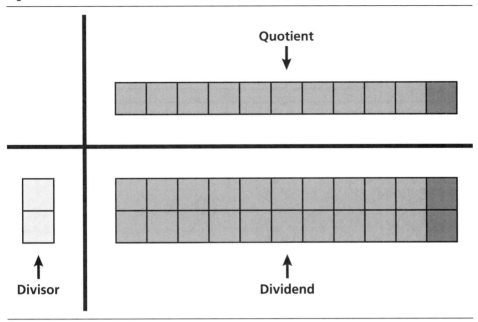

After working with the familiar bakery story to investigate division with and without remainders, we move on to the area model as another way to think about division. Exploration of division with the area model is often skipped in classrooms, but we must build the conceptual understanding of this model from the beginning because it is a model students will use throughout the upper elementary grades, middle school, and high school. Figure 7.12C shows an area model representation of 22 divided by 2. The lower left side (2 squares) represents the divisor, and the lower right part (22 squares) is the dividend. Students have to partition the dividend equally, building out the quotient (11 squares) above the dividend. If anything is left over, that is the remainder.

A math mat can provide other kinds of opportunities for students to make connections among the various models they have been working with. Students can talk about the math they are learning, reflect on what they know and what they still have to learn, and practice related vocabulary.

As the students conclude their exploration of division with and without remainders—which covers a number of models and strategies—they continue their focus on applying vocabulary properly in rich discussion. The closing division poster and recording sheet are shown in Figures 7.12D and 7.12E.

Figure 7.12D. Lesson 3. Poster: Reinforcement

MODELING DIVISION

$$52 \div 10 = 5\tfrac{2}{10}$$

EQUAL GROUPS

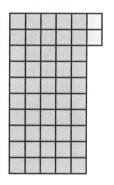

THINK MULTIPLICATION

$$10 \times \, ? \, = 50$$
(+ 2 more)

AREA MODEL

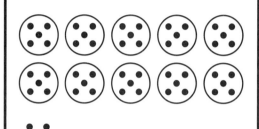

TAPE DIAGRAM

52

| 5 | 5 | 5 | 5 | 5 | 5 | 5 | 5 | 5 | 5 | 2 |

Remainder

OPEN ARRAY

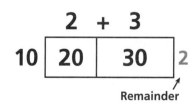

```
        2  +  3
   10 | 20 |  30  | 2
                    ↗
              Remainder
```

VOCABULARY

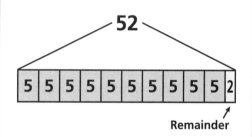

$$52 \div 10 = \, ?$$
Dividend   Divisor   Quotient

$$52 \div 10 = 5\tfrac{2}{10}$$
Dividend   Divisor   Quotient
with
remainder

Figure 7.12E. Lesson 3. Recording Sheet

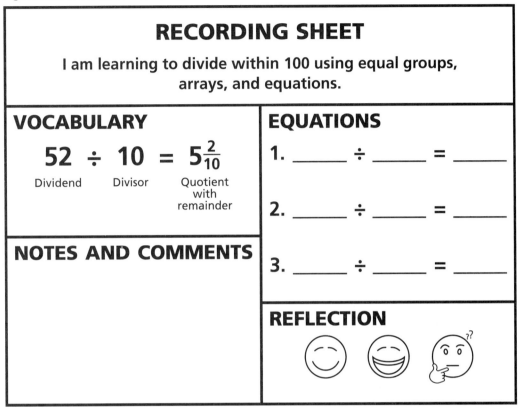

Overview of the Lessons

Throughout this series of lessons, students have tapped into prior knowledge and, as in many cases with intervention programs, we are building prior knowledge and then connecting it to the grade-level standards. All students deserve the right to learn on grade level. It can be done with the appropriate scaffolding. We must make sure that we provide many opportunities for them to make sense of and use the academic vocabulary and to explore, understand, and discuss multiple representations. Students should engage in math talk throughout the process so that they can listen to others and explain their own thinking. They also must be given the opportunity to reflect. We must embed these elements throughout our day-to-day lessons.

Figure 7.13. Quick Look Checklist: Cycle of Acceleration

Area of Intervention and Goal	Evidence of Need	Action Plan	Progress Monitoring: Quick Checks/ Assessments
• Learning goal • Success criteria	• Preassessment • Interview	• 2 weeks • 3 sessions/week • 20 minutes/session • 60 minutes/week	• Daily exit slips • Weekly reflections • End-of-unit assessments

LESSON PLANNING

There are many different ways to plan for acceleration. Lesson planning templates need to take into consideration certain critical points (see Figure 7.13). We have to document what we are trying to do and why we are trying to do it. What is our goal and what is the evidence of need? Exactly what is our action plan and how will we monitor it along the way? Mapping this out in advance for a cycle of acceleration will help us succeed in helping our students.

Two sample lesson planning templates are provided here. Additional examples appear in Chapters 6 and 8: Figures 6.17, 6.18, 8.18, and 8.19.

The lesson planning template shown in Figure 7.14 features a week-long format with spaces for noting the priority focus, the activities that will take place during the lesson, the learning goal written as an "I Am Learning" or "I Can" statement, and teacher observations.

Figure 7.15 shows a detailed lesson planning template. Included are spaces for the launch, vocabulary, specific prior knowledge the teacher will tap into, tools that will be used, guided aspects of the lesson, and independent practice activities. There is also space to plan the wrap-up and the reflection, as well as space for general comments. Spaces for teacher observations are also featured in this particular template.

PROGRESS MONITORING

It is important to monitor progress with spot checks throughout the unit of study so that we will know if we are on the right track with our intervention. Progress monitoring allows us to see what is working, what might need to be changed, and where there are still gaps. Progress monitoring also allows students to reflect on how their learning is developing, so they can set goals and work toward them.

In the examples that follow (see Figures 7.16–7.18), notice that students are asked to model their thinking, work with different models of the concept,

Figure 7.14. Lesson Planning Template

ACCELERATED MATH INTERVENTION LESSON PLAN				
Unit: _____ Week: _____	Priority/ Focus Standard	Lesson Activities	I Am Learning to/ I Can	Observations
Monday				
Tuesday				
Wednesday				
Thursday				
Friday				
Notes to Self/ Next Steps				

and discuss the concept in different ways, using numbers, words, and pictures. Students are also asked to talk about how they are feeling about the math. Remember that disposition is important and directly impacts motivation. We have to make sure we are monitoring how students are feeling about what they are learning, so we can make sure to give the encouragement they need along the way.

The recording sheets discussed above in the lessons include some examples of daily monitoring. Additional examples of monitoring follow: daily monitoring (Figure 7.16), weekly monitoring (Figure 7.17), and end-of-unit monitoring (Figure 7.18).

Figure 7.15. Lesson Planning and Observation Template

MATH INTERVENTION LESSON PLAN		
Interventionist: **Date:**	**Lesson:** **Focus:**	
Prior Knowledge:	**Manipulatives/Scaffolds:**	
Launch: • Tell me how you are all doing with this topic. • What do you think about division? • Take a piece of paper and write for 1 minute everything you know about division. Use words, pictures, and numbers.	**Student Activity:** • How do you all want to practice today? • Would you like to play a board game, card game, or dice game?	**Wrap Up:** • How do you want to show what you know? • You can either tell me or write it out.
Notes:		
OBSERVATIONS		
Student: **Understanding:** 1 2 3 **Notes:**	**Student:** **Understanding:** 1 2 3 **Notes:**	**Student:** **Understanding:** 1 2 3 **Notes:**

Scores: 1—Beginning
         2—Partially understands the concept/skill
         3—Fully understands the concept/skill		

Figure 7.16. Daily Monitoring: Exit Slips

Name: _____   Date: _____

EXIT SLIP

If there is a total of 24 apples and it takes 2 apples to make a mini-pie, how many mini-pies can be made?

?? Was this: EASY-PEASY   KINDA TRICKY

SOMEWHAT DIFFICULT

Name: _____   Date: _____

EXIT SLIP

Circle all the problems that have a remainder:

8 ÷ 3   6 ÷ 2   20 ÷ 10   15 ÷ 4

10 ÷ 2   12 ÷ 5   3 ÷ 3

?? Was this: EASY-PEASY   KINDA TRICKY

SOMEWHAT DIFFICULT

Name: _____   Date: _____

EXIT SLIP: Models and Equations

What division equation is shown by this model?

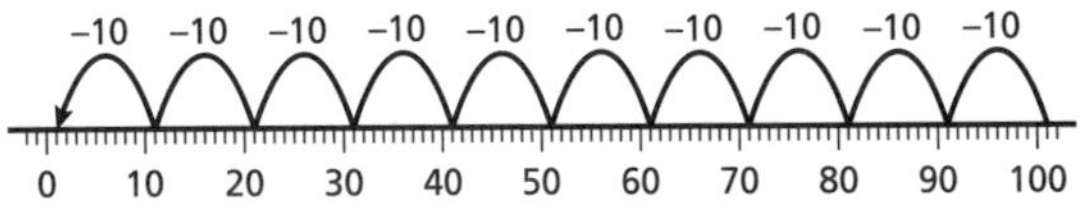

−10   −10   −10   −10   −10   −10   −10   −10   −10   −10

0   10   20   30   40   50   60   70   80   90   100

Name: _____   Date: _____

EXIT SLIP: Models and Equations

What division equation is shown by this model?

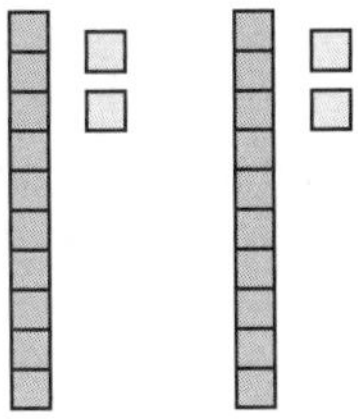

Figure 7.17. Progress Monitoring: End-of-Week 1 Quiz

DIVISION PROGRESS
A. Solve: $0 \div 3 =$ _____ $9 \div 1 =$ _____ $7 \div 7 =$ _____
B. Model this problem: $20 \div 5 =$ _____
C. What does this model show? Write the equation: 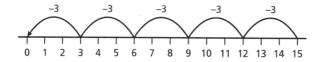 _____ $\div$ _____ $=$ _____
D. Write an equation for this model: ![number line with jumps of −3 from 15 to 0, marked 0–15]
E. Write about division. Use math words, models, and numbers.
F. How do you feel about learning division right now? Circle the face that shows how you feel.

Figure 7.18. Progress Monitoring: End-of-Week 2 Quiz

DIVISION CHECK-IN

Name:	Date:	Class:

Model this problem: **7 ÷ 3 =** _____	What does this model show? Write the equation. _____ ÷ _____ = _____ <table><tr><td colspan="4" align="center"> 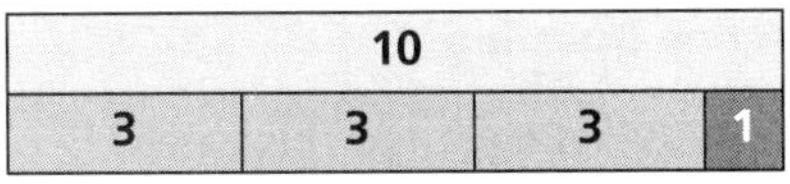10</td></tr><tr><td>3</td><td>3</td><td>3</td><td>1</td></tr></table>
Solve: **8 ÷ 3 =** _____ **25 ÷ 5 =** _____ **34 ÷ 3 =** _____	If Aunty Mary has 21 apples and it takes 5 apples to make 1 apple pie, how many apple pies can she make? _____ ÷ _____ = _____

POST-UNIT VOCABULARY CHECK-IN

What I know about this vocabulary word now!	 🙂	 😄	 🤔
Divisor			
Dividend			
Quotient			
Multiply			
Factor			

How well do you feel you understand the concept?
How will you continue to practice?
What do you need more help with?

REFLECTING ON THE ACCELERATION CYCLE

At the end of the acceleration cycle it is important to reflect on what happened. We begin with an itinerary and then we make the actual journey. We need to reflect on what worked well, what didn't work at all, and what might have worked better (see Figure 7.19).

Figure 7.19. Evaluating Acceleration

Reflection Question	Response
What lessons did you do this week?	*Lesson about division.* *3 major concepts: Dividing within 100; Dividing a 2-digit by a 1-digit; Dividing with remainders.*
Why did you choose those lessons?	*Because they followed a targeted trajectory of learning.*
How did you engage the students throughout the lessons?	*We did concrete, pictorial and abstract activities. We monitored progress along the way.*
How did you check for understanding throughout the lesson?	*Asked questions; Had students explain their work. Did understanding check-ins with response cards.*
What kind of guided practice did you give the students?	*We did a problem together. They did a problem with a partner. They did a problem on their own.*
How do you know they learned the concepts?	*I know they were practicing the concepts. I know that they are now more familiar with the concepts. They are learning the concepts. I can tell this by their level of work and their conversations.*
What is the evidence of learning?	*The workmat has evidence that they can use the designated models. The discussion also provides evidence of understanding. The reflection gives some insight as well.*
How did you incorporate academic language throughout the lesson?	*The language is previewed before the lesson, used throughout the lesson (on the workmat as well), and reviewed at the end of the lesson.*
What went really well?	*The students could picture what we were doing. The grid paper helps them to visualize the math.*
Would you do anything differently next time? Why or why not?	*I wish I had more days.*
Do you have anything else to add?	*We have to continue having students engage in meaningful practice at home.*

SUPPORTING THE ACCELERATION CYCLE

Throughout the unit Lucy will be provided targeted resources to help her practice the focus skills. She might use division bookmarks, charts, multiplication tables, visual flashcards, and strategy posters, and she might play board games to practice.

Division charts (see Figure 7.20) are another way for students to check their work in division. They are not as widely used as multiplication charts, but they are also great for looking at patterns. When students are playing games and they need a way to check their answers, these are great tools for doing that.

Figure 7.20. Division Chart

	÷1	÷2	÷3	÷4	÷5	÷6	÷7	÷8	÷9	÷10	÷11	÷12
=1	1	2	3	4	5	6	7	8	9	10	11	12
=2	2	4	6	8	10	12	14	16	18	20	22	24
=3	3	6	9	12	15	18	21	24	27	30	33	36
=4	4	8	12	16	20	24	28	32	36	40	44	48
=5	5	10	15	20	25	30	35	40	45	50	55	60
=6	6	12	18	24	30	36	42	48	54	60	66	72
=7	7	14	21	28	35	42	49	56	63	70	77	84
=8	8	16	24	32	40	48	56	64	72	80	88	96
=9	9	18	27	36	45	54	63	72	81	90	99	108
=10	10	20	30	40	50	60	70	80	90	100	110	120
=11	11	22	33	44	55	66	77	88	99	110	121	132
=12	12	24	36	48	60	72	84	96	108	120	132	144

Examples: 9 ÷3 =3   *and*   80 ÷10 =8

"I Can" Statements and Success Criteria

Displaying "I Can" or "I Am Learning" statements in very visible ways is important so that students can see, think about, and discuss and reflect on what they are learning (see Figure 7.21). Along with the learning goal, success criteria (see Figure 7.22) should be displayed so that students know what it looks like when they can meet the standard.

Board and Card Games

Board games are a great way to practice facts, once students understand the concept. Playing games is engaging and gives students repeated practice over time. Everyone can play a board game or a card game, and games can be easily differentiated. A variety of board games and card games are readily available (or can be invented) that students can play to practice (see Figure 7.23 for some examples). To differentiate in a lesson focusing on remainders, students might play a game that is straightforward, using facts to get from start to

Figure 7.21. "I Am Learning" Posters

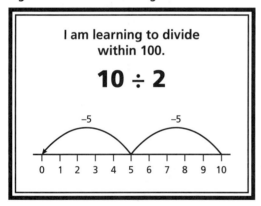

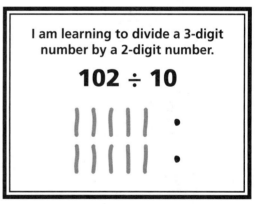

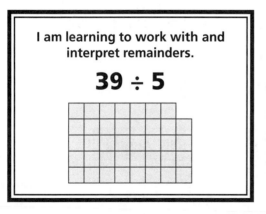

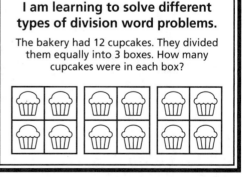

Figure 7.22. Success Criteria

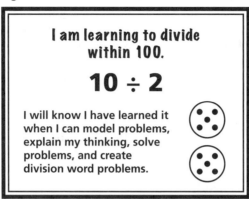

finish on a game board. You can vary the types of numbers, with some boards having more manageable numbers and problems students can visualize or can solve quickly with manipulatives. At the same time, another group of students could be playing a different board game focusing on remainders, but the numbers could be much larger and the problems more difficult. We want all students to be working on the grade-level standard and to be able to scale up in complexity as they become more secure with the concept.

Visual and Traditional Flashcards

Visual flashcards can be very useful. They can help students to see the concept of what they are doing and give them something to talk about. On the division flashcard shown in Figure 7.24A, one side has an example of partitive division and the other side has an example of quotative division. In this way, students can see the equation and examples of both types of division with a real-life problem.

The remainder flashcard shown in Figure 7.24B is also very helpful for scaffolding conversations about division. Students look at the model and decide what the equation is and what the remainder is. This helps with building conceptual understanding and gives students practice on solving word problems. Oftentimes it is good to include the answer on the back of flashcards so that students can self-check.

Figure 7.24C shows a pair of scaffolded flashcards that build fact family fluency. Students can talk about and come up with the different related facts by looking at the pictures and discussing them. Thus, they are building an understanding of how these facts are related. They first name the multiplication facts; then they name the related division facts. The card on the left shows 5 × 3 and 3 × 5; then it asks for the related division facts: 15 ÷ 5 and 15 ÷ 3. Once students have had plenty of opportunity to work with these concepts, they can then work with more abstract cards.

Figure 7.23. Division Board Games and Card Games

Focus of Game	Game
Basic division	**Traditional Board Game** Students move around the game board and answer the problems as they go. Whoever reaches the finish first wins. They can use whatever scaffolds they need during the game. 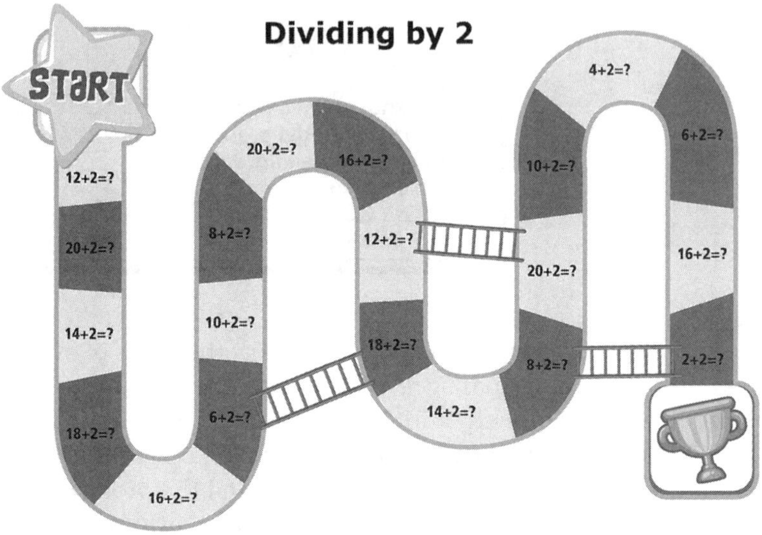 **Dividing by 2** START $4 \div 2 = ?$ $6 \div 2 = ?$ $10 \div 2 = ?$ $16 \div 2 = ?$ $20 \div 2 = ?$ $12 \div 2 = ?$ $12 \div 2 = ?$ $8 \div 2 = ?$ $20 \div 2 = ?$ $16 \div 2 = ?$ $20 \div 2 = ?$ $18 \div 2 = ?$ $8 \div 2 = ?$ $2 \div 2 = ?$ $10 \div 2 = ?$ $14 \div 2 = ?$ $14 \div 2 = ?$ $6 \div 2 = ?$ $18 \div 2 = ?$ $16 \div 2 = ?$
Basic division with remainders	**Card Games** Students pull a card and then tell a problem and write the equation. 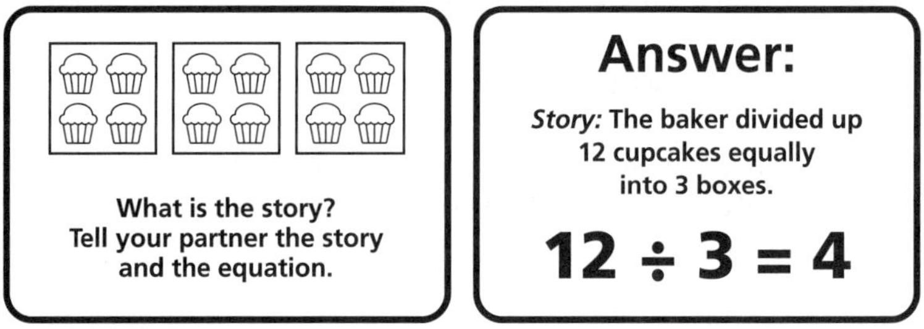 What is the story? Tell your partner the story and the equation. **Answer:** *Story:* The baker divided up 12 cupcakes equally into 3 boxes. **$12 \div 3 = 4$**
Equivalent expressions	**Advanced Card Game** These double-sided cards are great for practicing problem solving. There is a puzzle on the front and the answers on the back. Students look at the numbers and try to figure out equivalent expressions. On the back they see that $24 \div 6$ is equivalent to $20 \div 5$. 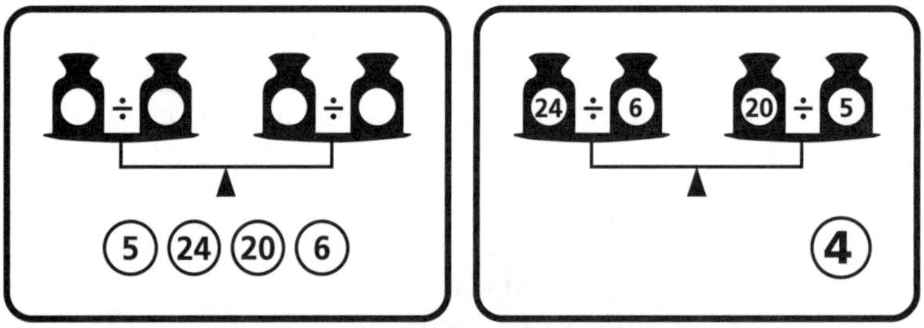 5 24 20 6 $24 \div 6$ $20 \div 5$ 4

The fact family flashcard shown in Figure 7.24D (front and back) is more traditional. Such cards are an important element in the toolbox because we want students to be able to think about the relationship between multiplication and division. These cards face front to back, so students look at the triangle (which is a very abstract representation) and then they have to state the four facts associated with this fact family.

Figure 7.24A. Division Game Flashcards

Equal Groups

15 ÷ 3 = ?

15 marbles divided among 3 kids.
How many marbles does each kid get?

Equal Groups

15 ÷ 3 = ?

15 marbles with 3 each in boxes.
How many boxes?

Figure 7.24B. Remainder Flashcard (front and back)
Answers appear on the back of this card. This allows students to self-check their responses.

Tom had 8 marbles. He divided them equally among 3 bags.

How many were left over?

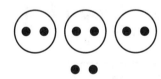

Tom put 2 marbles in each of the 3 bags.

2 marbles were left over.

Figure 7.24C. Fact Family Flashcards

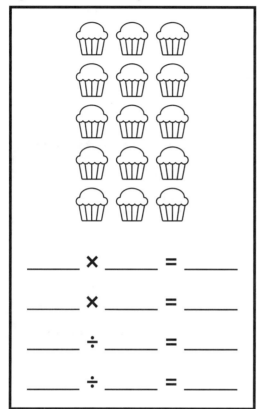

Figure 7.24D. Fact Family Flashcard (front and back)

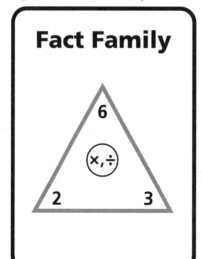

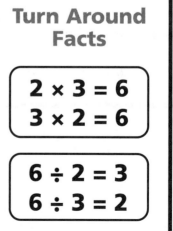

SUMMARY

An accelerated lesson cycle uses prior knowledge to bridge to future knowledge. Teachers must weave a pathway from the foundational information to the new knowledge by strategically reaching back to specific concepts and skills that relate to the current work. Some of the lessons are done to build on prior knowledge while others are done to explicitly connect the prior knowledge lessons to the current ones.

Students should be actively engaged as they work on vocabulary, content, and the strategies and skills that they need to know to be successful. There should be a big emphasis on making meaning with models so that students can feel and see the math they are doing. It is important that they not only look back and think about what they should be doing but also look forward to how they should be modeling their thinking. Make sure to give students time to reflect upon and think about their progress and to set new goals.

CHAPTER 8

Acceleration
A Middle School Example

In this chapter we will look at fractions, partly because fractions are the bane of the middle schooler's math existence. Students really struggle with fractions and often have a shaky understanding of fundamental concepts. In terms of math intervention, we have to think about the best ways to accelerate instruction by building background knowledge and tapping into the students' life experiences. Cramer and Whitney (2010) advise us to "Set building number sense for fractions among elementary school-aged students as a goal as opposed to building procedural skill with adding, subtracting [and dividing] fractions" (p. 21). We have all heard the adage "Ours is not to reason why, just invert and multiply!" Neagoy (2008) points out that this "Lack of sense making" is why our students are frustrated, demoralized, and unmotivated, and just give up on trying to learn fractions.

When we are accelerating lessons on fractions, we need to start with the known. We should do problem solving based on real-life scenarios that students can imagine, conceptualize, and act out. This is a steep climb because we are working not only on fractions but also on basic operations such as multiplication and division, which many intervention students are still learning. Scaffolding is key in the intervention lessons. Students might need multiplication and division charts and mats so that they are not cognitively overloaded. The daily 10-minute period of fluency practice (developing basic fact power) is also crucial.

In talking about division of fractions, Ma (1999) noted that "division is the most complicated of the four operations. Fractions are often considered the most complex numbers in elementary school mathematics. Division by fractions, the most complicated operation with the most complex numbers, can be considered as a topic at the summit of arithmetic" (p. 55). Fischbein et al. (1985) note that when students don't really understand basic division, it just gets more complicated when they are working with numbers less than one.

MARIO

Mario is a 6th-grade student. His class is working on division of fractions. However, Mario is struggling with fractions, and a preassessment showed that he has a shallow understanding of division too. The teacher will need to do a targeted trace at least back to 5th-grade standards. Mario still needs to work on his multiplication facts as well (a 3rd-grade standard).

Goal: To accelerate the teaching of dividing a fraction by a fraction.
The Standard: Dividing a fraction by a fraction.
How: Teach Mario the 5th-grade standards of dividing a unit fraction by a whole number and of dividing a whole number by a unit fraction. At the same time, make connections between what he is currently studying in school and the targeted prior standards so that he can learn the grade-level content. Mario will also need to continue to work on his mastery of the basic multiplication facts.
Plan: Give Mario a visual trajectory of what we will be working on (such as the one in Figure 8.1). Set out a 2-week intervention cycle of intensive learning sessions of 20 minutes each, 3 times a week. That will be a total of 60 minutes a week for 2 weeks. This will be the first round of acceleration lessons. The plan for these weeks appears in Figure 8.2.

LEARNING TRAJECTORY OF DIVISION

Mario is still struggling with understanding the concept and the procedures of division. He is wrestling with basic division within 100. The trajectory shown in Figure 8.1 will provide him with a visual map of the path to acquiring this foundational knowledge.

Progression of Learning in Division, Grades 3–6

The trajectory of learning division within 100 starts with understanding dividing 0 by a number, dividing by 1, and dividing a number by itself. Oftentimes, students have trouble understanding these basic concepts. Students also need to understand dividing by 2 and dividing a number by its half. For the rest of the division facts, students are encouraged to think about the related multiplication fact. Some students struggle with this because, although they know what strategy to use, they don't know their multiplication facts. After students have mastered dividing within 100 in 3rd grade, they go on in 4th grade to learn about dividing with remainders and then solving multidigit division problems.

As we think about learning fractions, we look at understanding what a fraction is, how to make equivalent fractions, and then how to operate with fractions. Students learn to add and subtract fractions, with like and unlike denominators. Then, they learn to multiply and divide with whole numbers and eventually with two fractions. In 6th grade, they are supposed to build on the knowledge and skills of dividing with unit fractions. Sometimes, students can do the problems procedurally but without understanding. It is important to bridge (and oftentimes build) their prior knowledge to the 6th-grade skills of dividing any fraction by whole numbers, dividing whole numbers by any fraction, and dividing fractions by fractions. These concepts must be built through contexts that make sense to students.

Figure 8.1. Division Learning Trajectory: Division Within 100

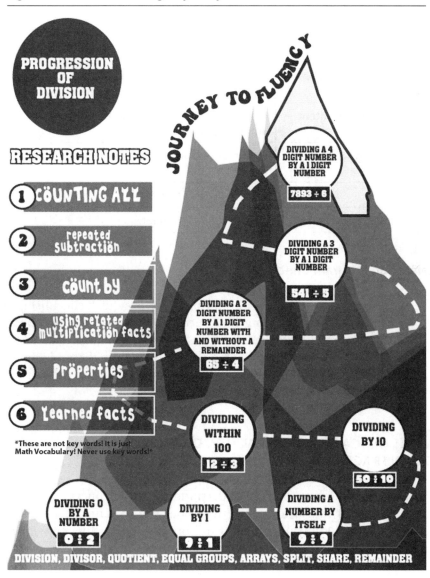

Figure 8.2. Accelerated Math Lesson Checklist

Stage	Topic/Activity
Clear Learning Goal	Learning to divide a fraction by a fraction
Success Criteria	Students will know they can do it when they can • Model a problem • Explain their answer • Solve word problems • Compute quotients • Create a problem to match an expression or equation
Engaging Launch	Story
Vocabulary	Dividend, Divisor, Quotient, Factor, Multiply, Equation, Fraction, Numerator, Denominator, Reciprocal
Review of Prior Content Skills Needed for This Concept	Review 5th-grade standards of dividing a fraction by a whole number and a whole number by a fraction
Connection to Current Content	Make an explicit connection between 5th-grade skills and 6th-grade skills
Progress Monitoring	Workmat (including reflection), Anecdotals, Writing prompts
Feedback	Checklists, Oral and written feedback
Student Check-In/Self-Reflection	On the reflection sheet

Acceleration Program Checklist

As we prepare for the work with Mario, we write a quick checklist (see Figure 8.2) that includes the learning goal, success criteria, launch, vocabulary, connections to prior knowledge, progress monitoring, feedback, and student self-monitoring components. Explicitly planning for these elements allows you to make sure you touch on each of them. It's easy to miss something if you don't plan for it.

TWO WEEKS OF SCAFFOLDING FRACTION DIVISION: BIG IDEAS IN FRACTIONS

In this unit we want to build understanding of the concept of fraction division. We want Mario to be able to model and explain fraction division in different ways. We want him to work on developing fluency with the basic division facts and then be able to transfer those concepts, skills, and strategies to fraction division. We will be working through a learning cycle of concrete, pictorial, and abstract lessons summarized in Figure 8.3.

Prior Knowledge/Schema. Figure 8.4 shows a trace for division by fractions through 6th grade. We can look forward and back to instantly see the coherence across grade levels. It is important to make connections with not only the specific skill but also the vocabulary and the models.

Scaffolded Practice. Mario will be given mini-posters, visual flashcards, and games to play at home to reinforce his learning (see Figures 8.25–8.30). He can also use these tools to reference and practice in the math workstations. In addition, Mario will be given multiplication and division mats and charts to scaffold his thinking. He can also refer to the visual trajectory that

Figure 8.3. Accelerated Learning Cycle: Dividing Fractions by Fractions

STEP 1 Assess specific knowledge, skills, and vocabulary for division of fractions. Do a trace for division of fractions. (Progressive so you start where students start having trouble.)

STEP 2 Go back through the targeted standard to teach the prior knowledge (content, strategies, skills). Trace division of fractions back through 5th grade. Make connections explicit.

STEP 3 Hands-on, standard-based, academically rigorous tasks and activities to address prior knowledge. Use fraction circles, pattern blocks, fraction tiles, and templates.

STEP 4 Connect current grade-level standard to prior knowledge. Engage in rich tasks and activities. Make connections explicit. Provide scaffolds to access current content as needed. Use division charts, multiplication charts, multiplication and division tables.

STEP 5 Discussion is built into the lesson.

Figure 8.4. Trace of Division by Fractions, Grades 1–6

6TH GRADE	Division is a designated fluency. Students should completely understand whole number division.	Divide a whole number by any fraction or divide any fraction by a whole number.	Divide a fraction by a fraction.
5TH GRADE	Understand and interpret fractional remainders in division. Solve division problems where the remainder is interpreted as a fraction.	Divide a whole number by a unit fraction or divide a unit fraction by a whole number.	Multiply a fraction by a fraction.
4TH GRADE	Find whole number quotients and remainders with up to 4-digit dividends and 1-digit divisors, using strategies based on place value, the properties of operations, and/or the relationship between multiplication and division.	Partition shapes into ½s, ⅓s, ¼s, ⅕s, ⅙s, ⅛s, 1⁄10s, 1⁄12s, and 1⁄100s.	Multiplication of a fraction and a whole number.
3RD GRADE	Work with unit fractions.	Partition shapes into ½s, ⅓s, ¼s, ⅙s, and ⅛s.	Fluently multiply and divide within 100, using strategies such as the relationship between multiplication and division or properties of operations.
2ND GRADE	Partition shapes into ½s, ⅓s, and ¼s.		
1ST GRADE	Partition shapes into ½s and ¼s.		

Note: These are standards from NGA and CCSSO (2010) and most current state standards. Texas and a few other states follow a different trajectory from what is shown here.

was given to him at the beginning of the intervention (see Figure 8.1) to see the through line of learning.

Keeping Track. Throughout each lesson, the teacher will keep track of what is happening while working with students to get them to play an active role in their own learning. The teacher will make anecdotal notes about student affect—how they feel at the beginning of the lesson and how they feel at the end of the lesson. What do they do when they get stuck? What is their perseverance like, and how can that inform the teacher's moves toward building a growth mindset? Are students comprehending and using math vocabulary? At the end of the lesson, the teacher will collect evidence of learning. This can take place in a variety of ways, including questions, work artifacts, and oral and written reflections.

Assessment/Progress Monitoring. It is important to monitor progress throughout the lesson and across lessons. At the end of every week, the teacher should give a quick assessment to see if the intervention is working or not. Depending on the data, the teacher might need to continue the course, change course and reinforce more of what is being taught, or change the goals to something else.

TRACKING A TWO-WEEK ACCELERATION CYCLE

Mario will start out tapping into the 5th-grade standards and work his way into the 6th-grade standards through a 2-week lesson sequence that can be seen in Figure 8.5. Sample forms that can be used with these lessons are included in this chapter.

Figure 8.5 provides an overview of the 6-lesson acceleration cycle. Each section begins with a description of what will be happening in the lesson,

Figure 8.5. Sequence of Acceleration Lessons

Lesson 1	Review dividing a whole number by a unit fraction (see Figure 8.6)
Lesson 2	Review dividing a whole number by any fraction (see Figure 8.8)
Lesson 3	Divide a unit fraction by a whole number (see Figure 8.10)
Lesson 4	Divide any fraction by a whole number (see Figure 8.12)
Lesson 5	Divide a fraction by a fraction (see Figure 8.14)
Lesson 6	Tell word problems involving division of fractions (actually, this is done throughout the cycle of learning; see Figure 8.16)

followed by a poster showing a story problem and a breakdown of the math concepts involved in solving it. Finally, a work mat is provided with an overview of the task, models that will be helpful in understanding the solution, vocabulary, and space for reflection. See Figures 8.6 through 8.17 (pages 149–160).

Lesson 1. Dividing a Whole Number by a Unit Fraction

In this lesson, students start in a problem-solving context. They act out the problem with manipulatives and then draw a representation. They are expected to use the math vocabulary. Students are asked to make a connection to the big idea and to do a reflection on their learning. This lesson reviews the 5th-grade division standard of dividing a whole number by a unit fraction.

Figure 8.6 is an example of an anchor chart (poster) that can be used in this lesson. It can be shown before or after the lesson and talked and worked through. Notice the anecdotal breakdown of what each number in the equation means. It is very important to help students understand what the numbers mean so that they can explain what they are doing. It is much easier to interpret the quotient when you can explain the problem. Students should act out the problems with visual models and explain what they are doing as they do it. They should use the lesson vocabulary throughout the discussion (see Figure 8.7).

Lesson 2. Dividing a Whole Number by Any Fraction

In this lesson, students explicitly tap into prior knowledge with visual models. The emphasis should be on what division means, and then on what we are doing when we divide a whole number by any fraction. The question is, "How many of this can we take out of that?" Throughout the review of the prior standards, we use different models, including circles, strips, squares, and so forth. We tell various stories about cutting up cakes and pies. Then, we sketch out what we did with manipulatives. We discuss the numbers and how to write the equations, so that students understand what they are doing. At the end, students reflect on how they feel they are doing with the concept.

In Lesson 2, we bridge into the 6th-grade standard of dividing a whole number by any fraction. Building on what we did in the previous lesson, connecting with how we were using unit fractions, we move on to use any fraction. We discuss the problem as well as the numbers and the words used to describe what we are doing. We also add the number line model into ways we can represent what is happening (see Figure 8.8). We continue to unpack the vocabulary and add reflections on how our understanding is going (see Figure 8.9).

As students are working with different models, they are encouraged to solve the stories and to begin to tell new stories using these models and more.

Models provide students something to hold on to as they tell their stories. As they move the pieces, they begin to make sense of the situation.

Lesson 3. Dividing a Unit Fraction by a Whole Number

Dividing a unit fraction by a whole number is more complicated to understand. Students have a hard time understanding what is happening and coming up with situations that match an expression. Contexts and manipulatives are essential to build that conceptual understanding and to show a way to reason through problems. Students can visualize something like half of a cake, pizza, or pie. Sharing a familiar concept with them allows them to access the thought process. They can actually see having to share a part of something among a few people. Teachers should ask students what they have to share in their daily lives and weave this into stories. Then they can interpret the quotient because it makes sense.

In Lesson 3, students are reviewing the 5th-grade standard of dividing a unit fraction by a whole number. They are working with models and drawings. The vocabulary, connection prompt, and reflection prompt are all embedded in the lesson.

Notice that in this lesson students begin by acting out the story and then sketching it. They are exploring the answer through symbolic representation (see Figures 8.10 and 8.11). We want students to understand the connections between concrete, pictorial, and abstract representations. They should be able to explain what is happening in the algorithm.

Lesson 4. Dividing Any Fraction by a Whole Number

In this lesson, students are learning the 6th-grade standard of dividing any fraction by a whole number. We have used a story to situate the problem in a real-life context. Students will make sense of the problem using manipulatives and the number line model (see Figure 8.12). The vocabulary, connection prompt, and reflection prompt are all embedded in the lesson (see Figure 8.13). We want students to be able to reason about this problem. If there are ¾ and this amount is being split among 3 people, then each person would get ¼.

Lesson 5. Dividing a Fraction by a Fraction

Throughout the discussion of Lessons 1–4, we have focused on reasoning about the problem through modeling and representation. In 6th grade, students are expected to know the algorithm for dividing a fraction by a fraction. We have to teach it with understanding. When we get to this point we have to stop and talk about what a reciprocal is and why we use it.

In Lesson 5, students are learning the 6th-grade standard of dividing a fraction by a fraction. We are using a real-life story and acting it out with manipulatives and then drawings (see Figure 8.14). The students have the vocabulary, connection prompt, and reflection prompt right on the workmat (see Figure 8.15).

As we work through the problem for this lesson, we want students to be able to think about different models, explanations, and strategies for solving it. We always start with accessible fractions so that students can visualize the story. This story can be acted out with cups and sugar, and we *want* students to act it out. Measure ⅓ cup so that it isn't just some abstract number. We want students to measure out ⅓ cup and then physically see how many ⅙ cups they can take out of it. Then we can talk about representing that operation in different ways. How might we sketch it? What is actually happening? What is the answer, and does it make sense? After we do this, we have students extend their thinking. If we had ⅔ cup of sugar, how many ⅙ cups could we take out? Why? How do you calculate that by reasoning?

Lesson 6. Telling Word Problems Involving Division of Fractions

In this lesson, students are learning the 6th-grade standard of being able to create a story about an expression. We are drawing on all they have learned in the previous lessons. We have differentiated levels of prompts for students to choose from. Each one of the choices has numbers that students can visualize to tell a story, and they can use manipulatives and drawings.

The lesson launches with an example that students work through while talking and making sense of the problem (see Figure 8.16). We then open up the problem so that students have to pick their problem, model it, explain what they did, and explain the quotient (see Figure 8.17). This brings together everything we have been working on in this acceleration cycle to make sure that students know and understand the math. They have conceptual understanding, procedural fluency, reasoning, strategic competence, and confidence.

Figures for Lessons 1–6 (Figures 8.6–8.17) follow.
The text continues on page 161.

Figure 8.6. Lesson 1. Poster: Dividing a Whole Number by a Unit Fraction

DIVIDING A WHOLE NUMBER BY A UNIT FRACTION

Aunty Mary made 2 mini-cakes. She split them into thirds. How many pieces did she get?

The number of ← $2 \div \frac{1}{3} = ?$ → How many total
cakes she had pieces she got

↓

The sizes she cut
the cakes into

START WITH ...

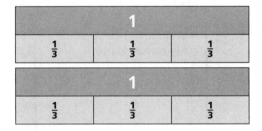

1 WHOLE

1 WHOLE

THEN ...

1		
$\frac{1}{3}$	$\frac{1}{3}$	$\frac{1}{3}$

1		
$\frac{1}{3}$	$\frac{1}{3}$	$\frac{1}{3}$

FINALLY ...

Count how many $\frac{1}{3}$s there are.

The number of ← $2 \div \frac{1}{3} = 6$ → How many total
cakes she had pieces she got

↓

The sizes she cut
the cakes into

Figure 8.7. Lesson 1. Math Mat: Dividing a Whole Number by a Unit Fraction

MATH MAT: Dividing a Whole Number by a Unit Fraction

I am reviewing how to use strategies to divide a whole number by a unit fraction.

Tapping into what we have studied before: Dividing a whole number by a unit fraction

• What is division?

• What does it mean to divide a whole number by a unit fraction?

The bakery cut 2 cakes into ⅛s.

• How many pieces did they get?

• What would the equation be?

Model the problem with fraction circles.	**Draw a sketch of the problem.**

Vocabulary	**This reminds me:**	**Reflection**
Division Numerator Denominator Fraction Unit Fraction Multiply Whole Number Quotient Divisor Dividend		

Figure 8.8. Lesson 2. Poster: Dividing a Whole Number by Any Fraction

DIVIDING A WHOLE NUMBER
BY ANY FRACTION

**Aunty Mary has 3 cups of sugar. To make a cake takes ⅔ cup.
How many cakes can she make?**

The amount ← $3 \div \dfrac{2}{3} = ?$ → How many cakes
of sugar she has   she can make

↓

The amount of
sugar it takes
for 1 cake

LINEAR MODEL

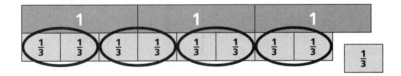

NUMBER LINE MODEL

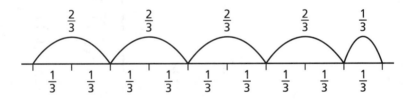

The amount ← $3 \div \dfrac{2}{3} = 4\dfrac{1}{2}$ → How many cakes
of sugar she has   she can make

↓

The amount of
sugar it takes
for 1 cake

Figure 8.9. Lesson 2. Math Mat: Dividing a Whole Number by Any Fraction

MATH MAT: Dividing a Whole Number by Any Unit Fraction

I am learning to use strategies to divide a whole number by any fraction.

Tapping into what we have studied before: Dividing a whole number by any fraction

- What is division?
- What does it mean to divide a whole number by any fraction?

Aunty Mary has 2 cups of sugar. To make a cake takes ¾ cup of sugar.

- How many cakes can she make?
- What would the equation be?

Model the problem with fraction bars.	Draw a sketch of the problem.
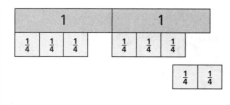	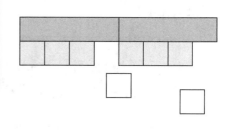

Vocabulary	This reminds me:	Reflection
Division Numerator Denominator Fraction Reciprocal Multiply Whole Number Quotient Unit Fraction		

Figure 8.10. Lesson 3. Poster: Dividing a Unit Fraction by a Whole Number

DIVIDING A UNIT FRACTION BY A WHOLE NUMBER

Aunty Mary had half a pan of brownies. She split it between her 2 grandchildren. How much did each child get?

The amount she started with ← $\frac{1}{2} \div 2 = ?$ → The fraction of the pan of brownies each child got

↓

The number of parts she partitioned the half pan of brownies into

AREA MODEL: FRACTION PATTERN BLOCKS

A way to show halves and fourths.

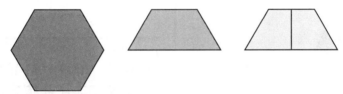

LINEAR MODEL: FRACTION TILES

A way to see the whole, then the half, then the half split into 2 parts.

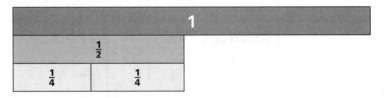

The amount she started with ← $\frac{1}{2} \div 2 = \frac{1}{4}$ → The fraction of the pan of brownies each child got

↓

The number of parts she partitioned the half pan of brownies into

Figure 8.11. Lesson 3. Math Mat: Dividing a Unit Fraction by a Whole Number

MATH MAT: Dividing a Unit Fraction by a Whole Number

I am reviewing how to use strategies to divide a unit fraction by a whole number.

Tapping into what we have studied before: Dividing a unit fraction by a whole number

- What is division?

- What does it mean to divide a fraction by a whole number?

Aunty Mary made a cake. She had ⅓ left. She shared it with her 2 grandchildren.

- What fraction of the cake did each child get?

- What would the equation be?

Model the problem with pattern blocks.	**Draw a sketch of the problem.**
 $$\frac{1}{3} \div 2 = \frac{1}{3} \times \frac{1}{2} = \frac{1}{6}$$	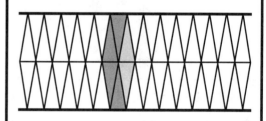

Vocabulary	**This reminds me:**	**Reflection**
Division Numerator Denominator Fraction Quotient Reciprocal Whole Number Multiply Unit Fraction		

Figure 8.12. Lesson 4. Poster: Dividing Any Fraction by a Whole Number

DIVIDING ANY FRACTION BY A WHOLE NUMBER

Aunty Mary had ¾ of a pan of brownies. She split it among her
3 grandchildren. How much did each child get?

LINEAR MODEL: FRACTION TILES

A way to see that ³⁄₁₂ is equivalent to ¼.

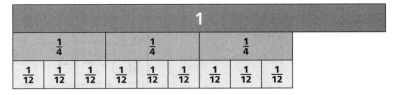

NUMBER LINE MODEL

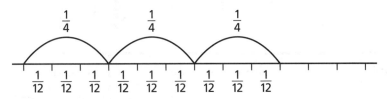

The amount she started with ← $\frac{3}{4} \div 3 = \frac{3}{12} = \frac{1}{4}$ → The fraction of brownie each child got

↓

The number of pieces of brownie she needed

Figure 8.13. Lesson 4. Math Mat: Dividing Any Fraction by a Whole Number

---

MATH MAT: Dividing Any Fraction by a Whole Number

I am learning to use strategies to divide any fraction by a whole number.

Tapping into what we have studied before: Dividing a unit fraction by a whole number

- What is division?
- What does it mean to divide a fraction by a whole number?

Aunty Mary had ⅔ of a pan of brownies left. She wanted to split it among her 4 grandchildren.

- What fraction of the brownies did each child get?
- What would the equation be?

Model the problem with fraction tiles.	**Draw a sketch of the problem.**

$$\frac{2}{3} \div 4 = \frac{2}{3} \times \frac{1}{4} = \frac{2}{12} = \frac{1}{6}$$

Vocabulary	**This reminds me:**	**Reflection**
Division Numerator Denominator Fraction Quotient Multiply Whole Number Unit Fraction		

Figure 8.14. Lesson 5. Poster: Dividing a Fraction by a Fraction

DIVIDING A FRACTION BY A FRACTION

Aunty Mary has ⅔ cup of sugar. She is is going to make mini-pies that require ⅙ cup of sugar. How many mini-pies can she make?

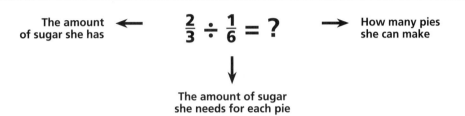

The amount of sugar she has ← $\frac{2}{3} \div \frac{1}{6} = ?$ → How many pies she can make

↓

The amount of sugar she needs for each pie

LINEAR MODEL: FRACTION TILES

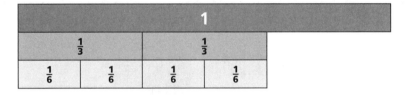

The amount of sugar she has ← $\frac{2}{3} \div \frac{1}{6} = 4$ → How many pies she can make

↓

The amount of sugar she needs for each pie

Figure 8.15. Lesson 5. Math Mat: Dividing a Fraction by a Fraction

MATH MAT: Dividing a Fraction by a Fraction

I am learning to divide a fraction by a fraction.

Tapping into what we have studied before: Dividing a fraction by a whole number and a whole number by a fraction

• What is division?

• What does it mean to divide a fraction by a fraction?

Aunty Mary is making cookies. She has ⅓ cup of sugar, and she needs ⅙ cup for each batch.

• How many batches can she make?

• What would the equation be?

Model the problem with fraction tiles.	**Draw a sketch of the problem.**
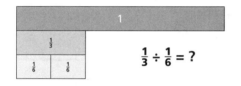	

Vocabulary	**This reminds me:**	**Reflection**
Division Numerator Denominator Fraction Multiply Quotient Whole Number Unit Fraction		☺ ☺ 🤔

Figure 8.16. Lesson 6. Poster: Telling Word Problems Involving Division of Fractions

WORD PROBLEMS: DIVIDING A FRACTION BY A FRACTION

Aunty Mary is making mini-cakes. She has ½ cup of sugar. If she needs ¼ of sugar for each cake, how many cakes can she make?

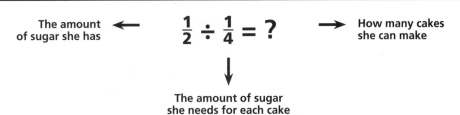

The amount of sugar she has ← $\frac{1}{2} \div \frac{1}{4} = ?$ → How many cakes she can make

The amount of sugar she needs for each cake

LINEAR MODEL: FRACTION TILES

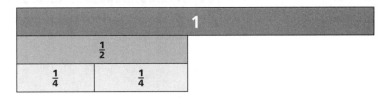

The amount of sugar she has ← $\frac{1}{2} \div \frac{1}{4} = 2$ → How many cakes she can make

The amount of sugar she needs for each cake

Figure 8.17. Lesson 6. Math Mat: Telling Word Problems Involving Division of Fractions

---

MATH MAT: **Telling Word Problems Involving Division of Fractions**

I am learning to tell word problems about fraction division.

Tapping into what we have studied before: Dividing a fraction by a fraction

• What is division?

• What does it mean to divide a fraction by a fraction?

Tell a story about:

$$\frac{1}{2} \div \frac{1}{4}$$ $$\frac{1}{3} \div \frac{1}{6}$$ $$\frac{2}{4} \div \frac{1}{8}$$

• What would the equation be?

• How will you model it? Fraction tiles, pattern blocks, fraction circles, number line?

Model the problem.	**Draw a sketch of the problem.**

Vocabulary	**This reminds me:**	**Reflection**
Division Numerator Denominator Fraction Quotient Multiply Whole Number Reciprocal Unit Fraction		

LESSON PLANNING

There are many different ways to plan for acceleration. A template provides a convenient starting point, and it can be more or less complex, depending on the needs and inclinations of the teacher. The important thing is that you *do* plan, in order to conduct the most effective interventions.

Two sample lesson planning templates are provided here. Additional examples appear in Chapters 6 and 7: Figures 6.17, 6.18, 7.14, and 7.15.

The acceleration map shown in Figure 8.18 has several components that serve as reminders of good practice for all intervention lessons. Each lesson should open with an organizer or routine that focuses on fluency. The map includes some options, but the main point here is to emphasize that you should use a variety of energizers; those listed are just some options. It is important that students work on fluency 10 minutes a day in your math intervention lessons (IES, 2009). The launch should always be well thought out and attention grabbing. The actual lesson should be interactive, engaging, focused, and rigorous. Always consider how you are connecting to real life and how you are integrating models throughout the lesson. Carefully consider how you are leading the students through concrete and pictorial experiences, and how you are connecting these to the abstract representation of the situation.

Figure 8.19 is an example of a different kind of lesson planning template. In this quick planner, there are spaces for the math power standards that will be the focus of the lesson, essential vocabulary, and prior knowledge connections. There is also space for any language frames that might scaffold talking about the math, as well as room to plan for manipulatives and any other scaffolds you might use. Finally, there are spaces to state what students need to know and what they need to be able to do by the end of the lesson.

PROGRESS MONITORING

Teachers should monitor student progress throughout the acceleration cycle (see Figures 8.20–8.23). In the lessons there has been an emphasis on modeling and explaining concepts. Visualization has been one of the key components of the intervention. Students should be able to see the target concepts and explain them. In the assessments, we want to see whether they can make sense of different representations, explain what they are doing, demonstrate procedural fluency, and think about their work in different ways. And we want to know if they are confident.

Progress Monitoring at the End of Week 1

Figure 8.20 shows a short monitoring quiz that can be administered at the end of the first week of the intervention. An early reading like this can let you

Figure 8.18. Acceleration Lesson Planning Template

MATH ACCELERATION LESSON PLAN FOR THE WEEK OF _____				
Monday	**Tuesday**	**Wednesday**	**Thursday**	**Friday**
I can divide a whole number by a unit fraction	I can divide a whole number by any fraction	I can divide a unit fraction by a whole number	I can divide any fraction by a whole number	I can divide a fraction by a fraction
Energizer/ Routines ☐ What Doesn't Belong? ☐ Vocabulary Tic-Tac-Toe/ Other Game ☐ Math Picture Chat ☐ Number Talk ☐ Bingo ☐ Other: _____	**Energizer/ Routines** ☐ What Doesn't Belong? ☐ Vocabulary Tic-Tac-Toe/ Other Game ☐ Math Picture Chat ☐ Number Talk ☐ Bingo ☐ Other: _____	**Energizer/ Routines** ☐ What Doesn't Belong? ☐ Vocabulary Tic-Tac-Toe/ Other Game ☐ Math Picture Chat ☐ Number Talk ☐ Bingo ☐ Other: _____	**Energizer/ Routines** ☐ What Doesn't Belong? ☐ Vocabulary Tic-Tac-Toe/ Other Game ☐ Math Picture Chat ☐ Number Talk ☐ Bingo ☐ Other: _____	**Energizer/ Routines** ☐ What Doesn't Belong? ☐ Vocabulary Tic-Tac-Toe/ Other Game ☐ Math Picture Chat ☐ Number Talk ☐ Bingo ☐ Other: _____
Launch	**Launch**	**Launch**	**Launch**	**Launch**
Activity ☐ Word problems ☐ Manipulatives/ Tools • Pattern blocks • Fraction squares • Fraction tiles • Fraction number lines ☐ Other: _____	**Activity** ☐ Word problems ☐ Manipulatives/ Tools • Pattern blocks • Fraction squares • Fraction tiles • Fraction number lines ☐ Other: _____	**Activity** ☐ Word problems ☐ Manipulatives/ Tools • Pattern blocks • Fraction squares • Fraction tiles • Fraction number lines ☐ Other: _____	**Activity** ☐ Word problems ☐ Manipulatives/ Tools • Pattern blocks • Fraction squares • Fraction tiles • Fraction number lines ☐ Other: _____	**Activity** ☐ Word problems ☐ Manipulatives/ Tools • Pattern blocks • Fraction squares • Fraction tiles • Fraction number lines ☐ Other: _____
Visualization ☐ Concrete ☐ Pictorial ☐ Abstract	**Visualization** ☐ Concrete ☐ Pictorial ☐ Abstract	**Visualization** ☐ Concrete ☐ Pictorial ☐ Abstract	**Visualization** ☐ Concrete ☐ Pictorial ☐ Abstract	**Visualization** ☐ Concrete ☐ Pictorial ☐ Abstract
Practice	**Practice**	**Practice**	**Practice**	**Practice**
Wrap-Up	**Wrap-Up**	**Wrap-Up**	**Wrap-Up**	**Wrap-Up**
Notes	**Notes**	**Notes**	**Notes**	**Notes**
More Thoughts				

Figure 8.19. Quick Lesson Planner

QUICK PLANNER	
Week of _____ Acceleration Group: Unit of Study:	Math Power Standard(s): Essential Vocabulary:
Prior Knowledge Connections: Language Frames:	Manipulatives: Other Scaffolds:
Students Need to Know:	Students Need to be Able to Do:

Figure 8.20. Progress Monitoring: End-of-Week 1 Quiz

DIVISION CHECK-IN		
Draw this: $3 \div \frac{1}{2}$	Circle the model below that shows this: $\frac{1}{4} \div 2$ 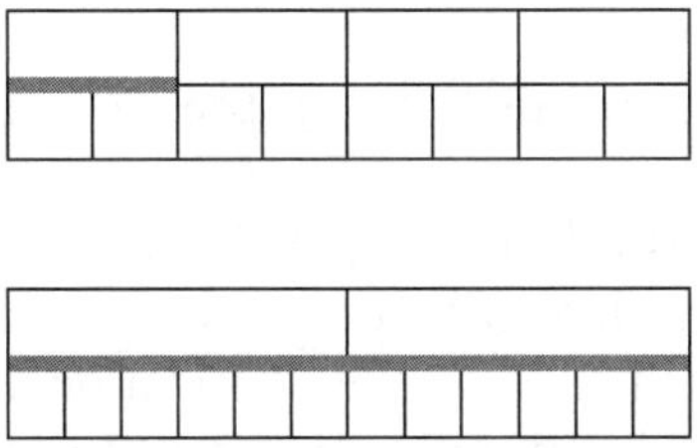	Aunty Mary had ½ of a cake left. She split it up between her 2 grandchildren. How much did each child get? Model: Equation:
What does it mean to divide a fraction? Explain it in your own words.	Draw a picture of how well you feel you understand the work so far.	

Figure 8.21. Exit Slips

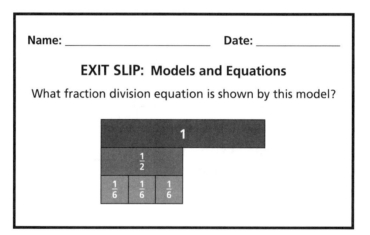

know if the students are picking up the material or if a change of course might be required.

Figure 8.21 shows two more examples of an assessment tool. These are quick exit slips that students fill out as they conclude a lesson. Exit slips might also ask students to tell a story about their model. Or they could ask students to model the same problem with a different representation.

It is important to have an item analysis sheet like the one in Figure 8.22 to help you quickly see where students are progressing and where they need more work. When using an analysis sheet, you want to consider not only what was done correctly and what was done incorrectly, but also what error patterns occurred. Why were the errors made? Are they conceptual errors, procedural errors, or reasoning errors? Ginsburg (1987) calls these kinds of mistakes "slips and bugs." Slips are careless errors and bugs are math errors. It is important to discover what students understand and do not understand so you can target their errors with specific, intentional interventions.

Figure 8.22. Data Analysis Sheet

ITEM ANALYSIS DATA SHEET

Topic: _____

SCORING GUIDE
1 — Fully understood
2 — Partially understood
3 — Doesn't understand yet

Student	Question 1	Question 2	Question 3	Question 4	Total Score

Progress Monitoring at the End of the Acceleration Cycle

At the end of the acceleration cycle, a summative assessment like the one in Figure 8.23 should always test students' knowledge, skills, modeling ability, and vocabulary. This information has been incorporated throughout the unit of study, so students should know all of these things by the end. In addition, the students' self-assessment provides important evaluation data (see Figure 8.23).

REFLECTING ON THE ACCELERATION CYCLE

At the end of the acceleration cycle, it is important to reflect on what happened. We begin with an itinerary and then we make the actual journey. We need to reflect on what worked well, what didn't work at all, and what might have worked better. A checklist like that in Figure 8.24 can help.

Figure 8.23. Progress Monitoring: End-of-Week 2 Quiz

	FRACTION DIVISION CHECK-IN	
Name: **Date:**		**Class:**

Solve: Aunty Mary had ⅔ cup of sugar. She wanted to make mini-pies that each needed ⅙ cup of sugar. How many mini-pies can she make?	Model and solve this: $\frac{2}{3} \div 4$
Model and solve this: $3 \div \frac{1}{2}$ **Quotient:**	Tell a fraction division problem to your teacher. Act it out with manipulatives. Write the equation.

POST-UNIT VOCABULARY CHECK-IN			
What I know about this vocabulary word now!	 🙂	 😄	 🤔
Divisor			
Dividend			
Quotient			
Multiply			
Factor			
Reciprocal			

How well do you feel you understand the concept?
How will you continue to practice?
What do you need more help with?

Figure 8.24. Evaluating Acceleration: Reflection Activity

Reflection Question	Sample Response
What lessons did you do during this acceleration cycle?	*Reviewed dividing a unit fraction by a whole number and a whole number by a unit fraction. We used this information to work up to dividing any fraction by any whole number and any whole number by any fraction and dividing a fraction by a fraction.*
Why did you choose those lessons?	*Because they followed a targeted trajectory of learning.*
How did you engage the students throughout the lessons?	*We did concrete, pictorial, and abstract activities. We monitored progress along the way. We used fraction circles, tiles, and pattern blocks.*
How did you check for understanding throughout each lesson?	*Asked questions. Had students explain their work. Did understanding check-ins with response cards.*
What kind of guided practice did you give the students?	*We did a problem together. They did a problem with a partner. They did a problem on their own.*
How do you know they learned the concepts?	*I know they were practicing the concepts. I know that they are now more familiar with the concepts. They are learning the concepts. I can tell this by their level of work and their conversations.*
What is the evidence of learning?	*The workmat shows evidence that they can use the designated models. The discussion also provides evidence of understanding. The reflection gives some insight as well.*
How did you incorporate academic language throughout the lesson?	*The language is previewed before the lesson, used throughout the lesson (on the workmat as well), and reviewed at the end of the lesson.*
What went really well?	*The students could picture what we were doing. Using the manipulatives and teaching through the telling of stories helped students to understand the concept.*
Would you do anything differently next time? Why or why not?	*I wish I had more days.*
Do you have anything else to add?	*We have to continue having students engage in meaningful practice at home.*

SUPPORTING THE ACCELERATION CYCLE

Throughout the unit, Mario will have a variety of targeted resources to help him understand and practice what he is studying. These might include flash-cards, strategy posters, board games, charts, and vocabulary support. These tools might be used during lessons, hung up in the classrooms, sent home, or kept in student notebooks for ready reference.

"I Can" Statements and Success Criteria

It is important that students know not only what they are doing but also what success looks like. They should be able to tell when they have learned the skills, strategies, and models to do the math. Having explicit success criteria helps students self-assess on an ongoing basis. In this way, they can seek extra help in problem areas, and they can enjoy a feeling of accomplishment when they meet goals. Displaying "I Can" statements and success criteria posters in the classroom (see Figures 8.25 and 8.26) is a student-friendly way of convey-ing success criteria.

Figure 8.25. "I Can" and "I Am Learning" Statements

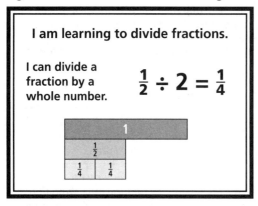

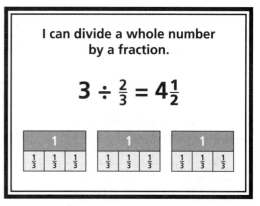

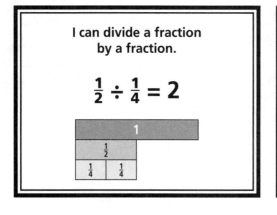

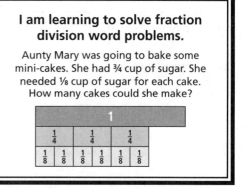

Anchor Charts

Anchor charts help reinforce what students are learning. Posters such as the one in Figure 8.27, for example, show different representations of how students might approach a problem.

Figure 8.26. Success Criteria

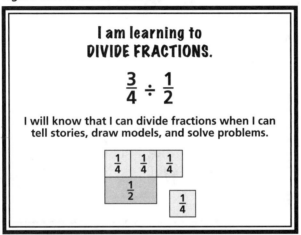

Figure 8.27. Fraction Division Poster

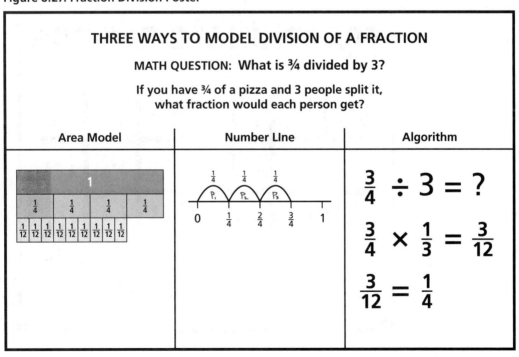

Figure 8.28. Differentiated Board Games and Cards

Focus of Game	Game
Conceptual understanding	**Modeling Activity** What is the expression for each of these models? How did you figure it out? 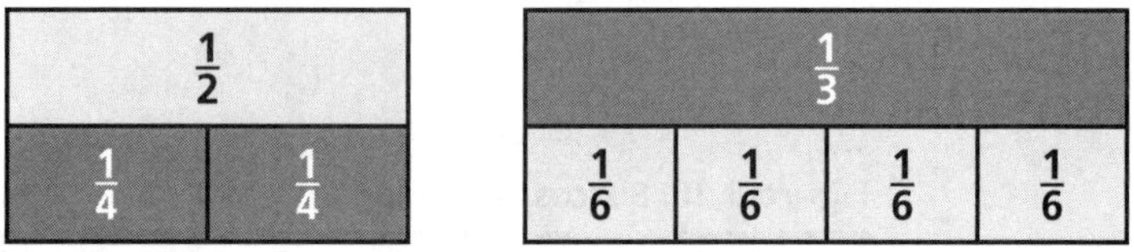
Reasoning	**Reasoning Flashcard** ¼ divided by ⅛ 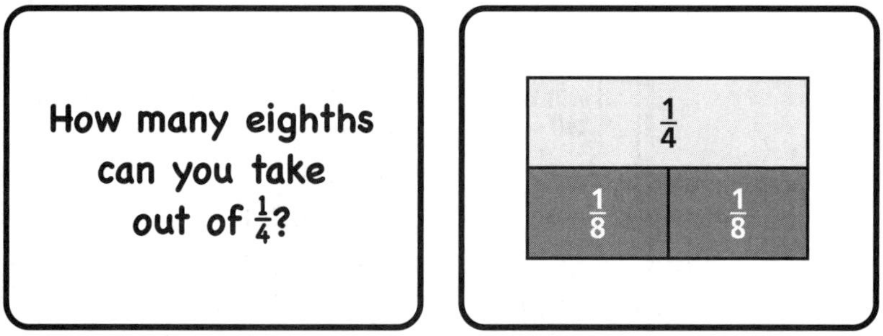
Procedural understanding	**Tic-Tac-Toe Board Game** 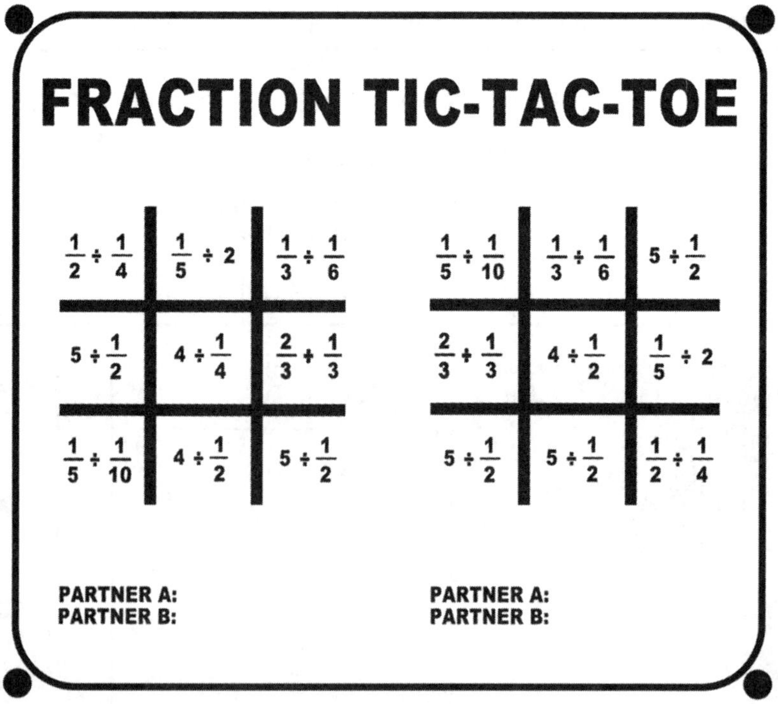

Board Games, Card Games, and Other Activities

Students should play games and engage in thinking activities throughout the unit of study. Figure 8.28 shows examples of activities that can strengthen student understanding. In an activity focused on conceptual understanding, students are asked to reason about a model, explain their thinking, and write the equation illustrated by the model. In a flashcard focused on reasoning, they are expected to reason without the pictorial scaffold, although they might draw their own sketch. The answer is given on the back side of the card (shown on the right in the figure). A traditional board game focuses on procedural understanding. Tic-tac-toe is a game structure students understand and can start playing right away. As they play, they can use manipulatives and sketches to help them think through problems.

Visual and Traditional Flashcards

Visual flashcards help students visualize the math they are doing. These are temporary scaffolds that may eventually be phased out, but while in use they can help students think about the math they are doing and practice math facts. They work equally well in the classroom and at home. Figures 8.29 and 8.30 show examples of visual and traditional flashcards.

SUMMARY

The key to acceleration is intentionally tapping into prior knowledge. In many cases, teachers need to *build* the targeted background knowledge (because students don't really remember what was taught earlier) and then connect it to the current lesson. In such a cycle, the teacher makes sure students have a firm grasp of the big ideas that come right before their current grade-level standard. Students should be an active part of the process. Division is a tough

Figure 8.29. Visual Fraction Division Flashcards

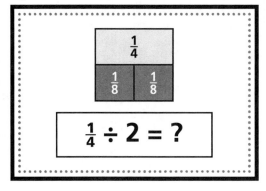
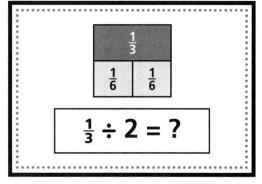

Figure 8.30. Traditional Fraction Division Flashcards

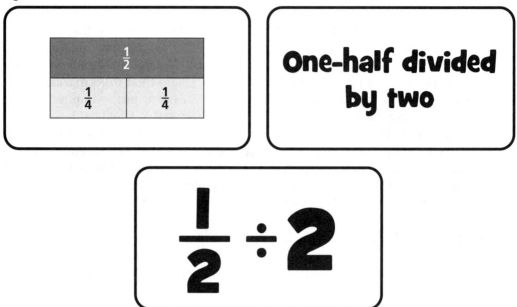

topic for students to understand. Math skills are cumulative, and higher-level concepts can be really difficult for students who are missing building blocks along the journey.

The key is to tap into how a targeted concept is a part of students' everyday lives. Division in the abstract is one of those topics that can give students a lot trouble. But if students can develop ongoing routines around division and fractions that draw from real life, they are much more likely to succeed. Problem solving is integrated throughout the acceleration process. Students should be able to act out real problems, sketch a drawing of their model, and discuss the meaning of their results. They should also be able to solve and create word problems.

CHAPTER 9

Connecting Progress Monitoring, Goal Setting, and Motivation

Students can hit any target that they know about and that holds still for them.

—Stiggins (2007)

PROGRESS MONITORING FOR ACCELERATION

One of the eight recommendations for math intervention (first discussed in Chapter 5) is progress monitoring. As noted in Chapters 6, 7, and 8, when teachers are working with students in acceleration lessons, they should monitor progress consistently. This is how we know what to do next. Progress monitoring helps us know whether the intervention is working or whether we need to make changes. Based on the information obtained, we can make instructional decisions. Progress monitoring should be done informally throughout intervention lessons, and formally on a weekly basis. It cannot be done only at the beginning and end of the intervention cycle.

Assessment is another integral part of the teaching cycle. It must be woven throughout every lesson in many different ways. Davies (2007) points out that "Anything a student says, does, or creates is potential evidence of learning." We must be sure to capture this evidence during our lessons. Documenting observations and anecdotals using formats like those offered in previous chapters, noting everything that happens, is important. Guskey (2007) points out that "Our assessment practices reflect our beliefs about the use of feedback to improve instruction." Formative classroom assessment is one of the most important factors in improving student achievement. It gives both teachers and students information about how the journey is going.

In progress monitoring and assessment, it is important to use a variety of question types, including selected response types (multiple choice, true/false, matching, and fill-in items where students select an answer from a provided list) and constructed response types (both short response and extended response) (Ainsworth, 2007). Figure 9.1 shows criteria teachers can use to quickly judge the quality of the tools they are using for formative monitoring of student progress.

Figure 9.1. Characteristics of High-Quality Progress Monitoring

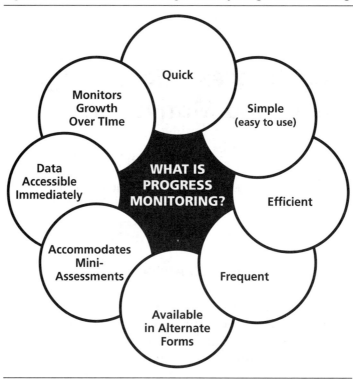

Throughout the intervention process, teachers need to ask themselves questions such as these:

- Are the interventions working?
- What's working?
- What's not working?
- What do we need to zero in on?
- Given what is happening, what are the next steps?

Evidence obtained from progress monitoring enables teachers to make instructional decisions and report on student growth, as shown in Figure 9.2.

When we monitor progress, research shows that students learn more, teachers can plan more effectively, teachers become better instructional decision-makers, and students become more aware of their performance (Safer & Fleischman, 2005). Figure 9.3 shows an example of use of a bar graph in progress monitoring for a 2nd-grader who is working on basic math fact fluency. The student is making progress, but we need to consider how the work is going on learning to add within 10, because the student has been at that level for 3 weeks. It might be time to do something differently to help the student with these facts.

Part of progress monitoring involves visually tracking data (IES, 2009; IRIS Center, 2021). Marzano (2007) and many other researchers suggest that students track their own progress on each learning goal. In the example shown in Figure 9.4, the dotted line (the aimline) represents progress goals and the solid line shows the student's actual progress (National Center on Intensive Intervention, n.d.). Students can be given blank ½-inch-scale graph paper to monitor their own progress. If after three sessions the data points are above the aimline, the teacher should adjust the aimline to a higher goal. If after three sessions, the student's progress line doesn't really go up and stays below the aimline, instruction should be adjusted to meet the ongoing needs of the student. If after three sessions, the data points are near the aimline, the intervention should continue on its current path.

This kind of self-monitoring system enables students to see their own progress as well as gain real-life experience with graphing. It can also motivate them and give them ownership of their learning journey (Benedict, 2020). Researchers have found that graphically displaying student data helps teachers see the information in different ways and better understand it. They can then make powerful instructional decisions that can raise student achievement significantly (Fuchs & Fuchs, 1986). Students are motivated by graphing their own data and being a part of the goal-setting process (Li, 2017).

Figure 9.2. Analyzing and Using Progress Monitoring Data

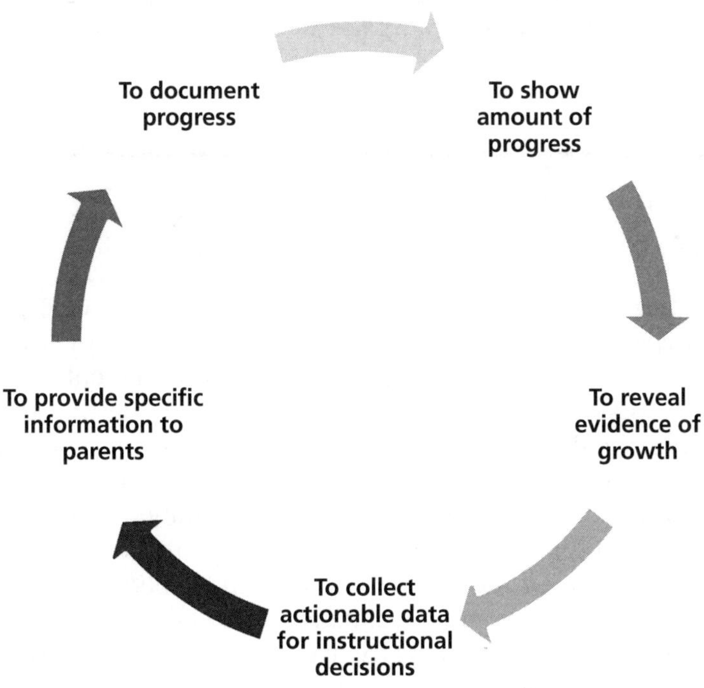

Figure 9.3. A Six-Week Progress Goal for 2nd-Grade Fact Fluency

Name: _____

LEARNING MULTIPLICATION FACTS WITHIN 10						
Make 10 Facts						
Add Within 10						
Make 5 Facts						
Zero Facts						
	Week 1	**Week 2**	**Week 3**	**Week 4**	**Week 5**	**Week 6**

GOAL SETTING

Goal setting can directly impact motivation. James (2019) points out that "Because your brain has something called neuroplasticity, goal-setting literally changes the structure of your brain so that it's optimized to achieve that goal." Csikszentmihalyi (1997) notes that goal setting and working toward those goals motivates us. Here is where co-constructing criteria and goal monitoring can be so powerful. Students are motivated when they see themselves making progress. Part of the acceleration process must be to set specific, realistic, scaffolded goals that students can work toward and achieve. We can draw on the theory of Nakamura and Csikszentmihalyi (2009) that when there is an appropriate challenge level coupled with the skill to do it and clear goals with immediate feedback, then we find our flow. Students can become engaged and enjoy the learning.

Figure 9.4. Student Progress Graph

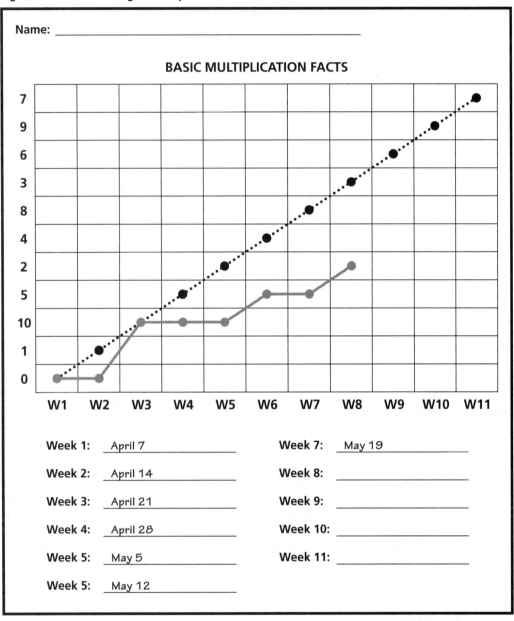

Davies (2007) states that we should set small goals so that students can have a sense of accomplishment along the way. In this regard, math fact fluency maps are extremely helpful. Students get to see the journey and feel the accomplishment on their way to all the things they need to learn. Figure 9.5 shows an example of a fluency map that allows students to visualize the trajectory of their learning and monitor their progress as they learn their addition facts.

Figure 9.5. Fluency Progression

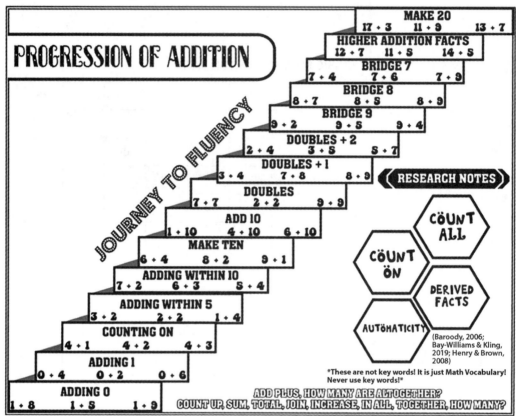

Working with students to establish goals that are achievable, relevant, and timely improves student achievement (Echevarría & Graves, 2007). Research shows that there is a strong connection between goals, motivation, and student improvement. Schmoker (1999) says that "good faith efforts to establish goals and then to collectively monitor and adjust actions toward them produce results" (p. 2). When students are working toward goals, there is a plan and it makes sense to both teachers and students.

STUDENT GOAL SETTING

Students need to be an active part of the goal setting process. We need to discuss the goals with our students and make a plan. Students need to take ownership of their goals and record them using templates such as those shown in Figure 9.6.

HIGH-QUALITY FEEDBACK AND MOTIVATION

Throughout an accelerated lesson cycle, teachers should be doing ongoing assessments that give them feedback about how their teaching is going, what needs to stay the same, what needs to change, and why. These assessments should also tell the teacher where the students are on the learning journey and what to do next. Teachers should give assessments that are quick to look over and easy to use to make instructional decisions. We must be able to make determinations about the knowledge, understanding, and skills that students are acquiring through the intervention. Guskey (1997) points out that when we give an assessment, the next move is to give high-quality corrective instruction to help students move forward. The research clearly states that descriptive feedback helps students grow and learn. We should have multiple data points, including interviews, self-assessments, exit slips, student work, and formal tests so that we can evaluate a body of work around the topic. Teachers need to "define learning destinations so students understand the goals they seek to achieve" (Davies, 2007).

The research shows that when students are motivated by what they are learning and involved in the assessment process, they learn more (Black & Wiliam, 1998; Falchikov, 2004; Ryan, 2019). Marzano (2007) notes that feedback should let students know exactly how they are doing and what they need to do to improve. Hattie (1992) found that "the most powerful single modification that enhances achievement is feedback. The simplest prescription for improving education must be 'dollops'" of feedback (p. 9). The quality of feedback that teachers give is crucial. Marzano (2006) notes that we must give feedback in a way that encourages students to keep trying. He argues that feedback must encourage students and help them to realize that their effort and perseverance matter and make a difference.

Figure 9.6. Student Goal Setting Template

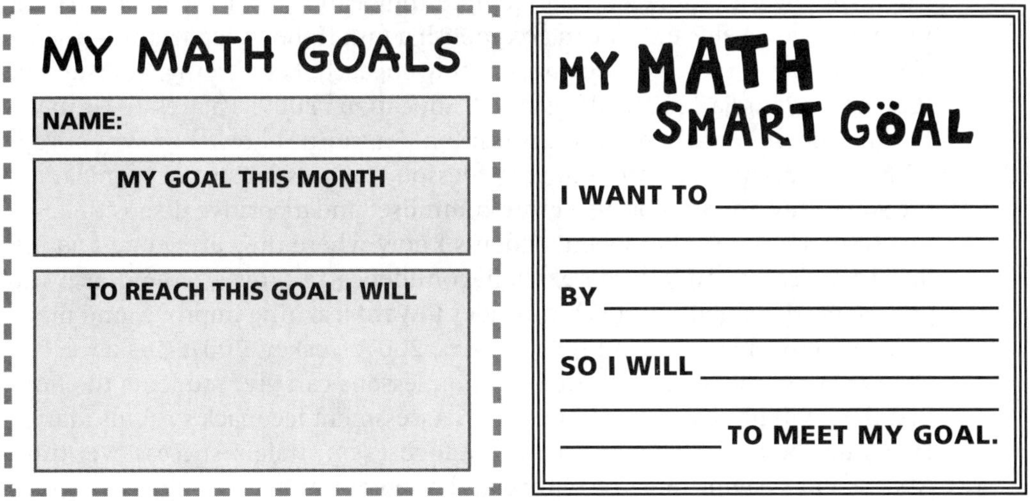

Teachers need to create several opportunities for students to receive feedback from multiple sources so that they can "feed-forward" their learning. Davies (2007) says that we must multiply the feedback effect by getting feedback from a variety of sources (parents, peers, other teachers). Davies (2007) also argues that students should be a part of the entire feedback process. Students should help select the assessment criteria, collect data, present evidence of learning, and reflect on what they are doing well with and what is challenging them so far. Davies (2004) argues that when students do this "they learn more, achieve at higher levels, and are more motivated." When students are involved in the learning process, they are engaged, connected, and invested in what they are doing (Davies, 2004). When you know where you are going you are much more likely to get there. Students need to understand the goals, and the goals should be clear and defined. Goals should be discussed, reflected upon, and acted on.

MOTIVATION AND GROWTH MINDSET

Roberts (2018) points out that as teachers design curriculum and lessons, they must ask themselves: How do I want students to feel? Students are always monitoring what they say out of fear of peer reactions (Sousa & Tomlinson, 2011). Sousa and Tomlinson point out that this fear shapes the discourse of the group. It is important to watch for and facilitate conversations and what happens when someone gives an incorrect answer. We have to establish norms in the math intervention group that everyone has the right to change their mind. Furthermore, mistakes help us learn. Posters like the one shown in Figure 9.7 can ensure that the message is front and center. Smaller versions can be given to students as bookmarks.

Sousa and Tomlinson (2011) also found out that students are encouraged by positive feedback from teachers and students, and that they will persevere when they feel encouraged and feel like they can do it if they keep trying. When students believe they can accomplish a task if they keep trying—a sense of self-efficacy—they feel encouraged, stay engaged, keep trying, and succeed (Levine & Pantoja, 2021; Ministry of Education, 2009; Pajares & Graham, 1999). Students' mathematical disposition determines how they will engage with the curriculum. Throughout the lesson teachers must stay cognizant of the ways they are promoting a growth mindset and a positive disposition.

Research shows that when students know where they are going and feel like they really can get there, their confidence improves, attendance improves, participation improves, attitudes toward learning improve, and many other affective measures improve (Davies, 2007; Guskey, 2007; Guskey & Pigott, 1988). Accelerated math intervention lessons can give students the hope that they will be able to learn the math. Assessment feedback systems matter. They must be constructed in a way that focuses on student success over time. Assessment systems must recognize and celebrate success (Marzano, 2007).

Figure 9.7. Healthy Mistake Message

Research on math intervention has identified three specific types of motivational awards (IES, 2009), as outlined in Figure 9.8 (on the next page). The first type of award is based on engagement. Students are attentive and participating in the learning. The second type of award is based on persistence. Students stick with it. They don't give up, and they keep trying until they get it. The third type of award is based on achievement. Students have finally made it, and this "making it" is celebrated.

SUMMARY

Progress monitoring is an essential part of accelerating math lessons. Assessing and giving feedback is part of the cycle of learning. How we give feedback makes all the difference. It determines whether our students stay motivated and keep trying and learning or whether they just throw in the towel, lose motivation, and give up. Teachers must stay cognizant of the importance of motivation. Research tells us that when students are motivated they will stick with the work, and when they stick with it long enough they will get it. This is why we accelerate—so everyone will feel successful and sooner or later will succeed.

Figure 9.8. Three Types of Motivational Awards

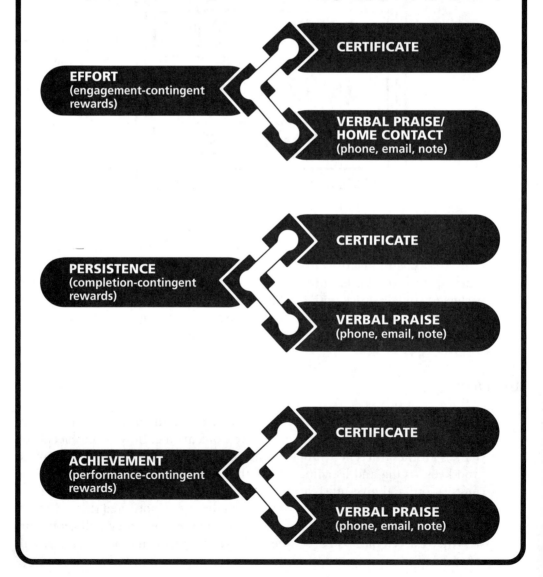

MOTIVATION

"Praising students for their effort and for being engaged as they work through mathematics problems is a powerful motivational tool that can be effective in increasing students' academic achievement. Tier 2 and Tier 3 interventions should include components that promote student effort (engagement-contingent rewards), persistence (completion-contingent rewards), and achievement (performance-contingent rewards)" (IES, 2009).

EFFORT
(engagement-contingent rewards)

> **CERTIFICATE**

> **VERBAL PRAISE/ HOME CONTACT**
> (phone, email, note)

PERSISTENCE
(completion-contingent rewards)

> **CERTIFICATE**

> **VERBAL PRAISE**
> (phone, email, note)

ACHIEVEMENT
(performance-contingent rewards)

> **CERTIFICATE**

> **VERBAL PRAISE**
> (phone, email, note)

Acceleration in Action
A Classroom Example

Christine King
Math Consultant, CKingEducation

I was working in a K–5 school and had just walked into a classroom designated as a 12:1:1. This is a designation given to small-setting special education classes, where there are a maximum of 12 students, 1 certified special education teacher, and 1 teaching assistant. I noted that the students who were working with the certified special education teacher were working on adding and subtracting with decimal amounts. As this was a 5th-grade class, that was to be expected. As I ventured further into the classroom I spotted a group of four boys, all boys of color. They were diligently working on adding 2-digit numbers. Upon seeing this, I pulled the teacher aside and asked, "If you are working on adding and subtracting with decimals, which is a 5th-grade standard, why is that group working on 2-digit addition, which is a 2nd-grade standard?" She looked over at the group and without thought to the ramifications, she loudly responded, "Because that's what they can do . . . 2nd grade . . . they need practice." Knowing that I was not going to be able to address her academic soul-killing declaration at that moment, I simply asked, "Would you mind if I worked with them?" To which she responded, "Sure. Knock yourself out."

I gathered some materials that she had on hand: two-colored counters, play coins, . . . , dollar bills, dimes, and pennies. I drew a place-value mat with ones, a decimal point, tenths, and hundredths on a dry erase board. I asked the boys if I could work with them. They were happy to have an adult—and a visitor at that—pay attention to them. I asked them what I had drawn on the dry erase board. They said, "A place-value chart." I asked them if they knew the labels (the units) as I pointed to them. They knew the ones, but they told me that that I placed the tens in the wrong place—that it was backward. I drew in the tens column and told them that the place value to the right of the ones was actually the tenths place, like dimes, and showed them a dime. I wrote the word dimes in parentheses right above the tenths label. I asked them what they thought this unit was as money as I pointed to the hundredths place-value column. One boy tentatively said "Pennies," while another student shouted out "Hundreds." I showed where the hundreds would be on the place-value chart and confirmed that the hundredths were indeed like pennies.

So far this had taken only about 1 to 2 minutes. I then used the two-colored counters as place-value discs. I placed 1 disc in the ones place, 2 discs in the tenths place, and 3 discs in the hundredths place. I told them that we say "and" when reading the decimal point, as the point represented a part of the whole unit. Like dimes and pennies are a part of a dollar. We practiced reading the decimal amount represented by the place-value discs, 1.23. As they read I pointed to the chart supporting where they got stuck. They knew to say, "One and twenty-three," but they did not know how to complete the amount. So I said the number fully as I pointed to each digit in the place-value chart and then pointed to the last label in the chart where the number terminated. I told them that when we read decimal amounts we read the number after the decimal point as we would any other amount, but we must say the unit indicated by the last place in the place-value chart.

After this, I gave the students a chance to create their own decimal numbers and read them to each other. We were about 6 minutes into our conversation. At that point, the students could name the decimal places to hundredths using the scaffold of the place-value chart, and they could read the amounts like money and as decimals.

I knew they were ready to add decimals. I knew this because I had observed them adding 2-digit whole numbers using the traditional standard algorithm. Using the other side of the two-colored counter I created another decimal amount underneath the first decimal amount and told them that we were going to add the amounts. The place-value discs represented the expression 1.23 + 1.45. The addends purposefully did not need regrouping.

The boys were hesitant for about 10 seconds and I said, "You can do this. It is the same thing you were doing with the whole number, but now you are working out decimals, like adding money." The boys talked and came up with 2.68. They looked up to me hesitantly and asked, "Are we right?" I said, "Are you?" They said, "Well, 3 and 5 make 8." I asked, "3 what . . . what is the unit?" They said, "3 pennies, 3 hundredths." I asked them to repeat their explanation using the unit labels as shown in the place-value chart. They did and knew that they were correct. I set up some more problems for them to try, model out, and justify their thinking with. The problems came from the worksheet that they had been working on with 2-digit whole numbers, but we just used the digits in decimal places. After about 15 minutes, one student shouted out as he beamed and his eyes sparkled, "We are doing 5th-grade math! We are really doing 5th-grade math!

References

Adventures of a Schoolmarm. (n.d.). *Schema maps.* Retrieved January 26, 2022, from https://www.classroomtestedresources.com/2016/01/schema-maps-great-alternative-to-kwl.html

Ainsworth, L. (2007). Common formative assessments: The centerpiece of an integrated standards-based assessment system. In D. Reeves (Ed.), *Ahead of the curve: The power to transform teaching and learning* (Kindle ed.). Solution Tree.

The All-Access Classroom. (n.d.). *How to unlock prior knowledge & boost students' comprehension.* https://www.theallaccessclassroom.com/prior-knowledge/

Almarode, J., Fisher, D., & Frey, N. (2021). *How learning works: A playbook.* Corwin.

Almarode, J., & Piccininni, S. (2019). *Direct instruction is not the enemy.* Retrieved February 5, 2021, from https://corwin-connect.com/2019/08/direct-instruction-is-not-the-enemy/

Almeida, L. (2007). The journey toward effective assessment for English language learners. In D. B. Reeves (Ed.), *Ahead of the curve: The power of assessment to transform teaching and learning* (Kindle ed.). Solution Tree.

Ambrose, S. A., Bridges, M. W., DiPietro, M., Lovett, M. C., & Norman, M. K. (2010). *How learning works: 7 research-based principles for smart teaching.* Jossey-Bass.

Anderson, J. (2020). *Harvard EdCast: Learning loss and the coronavirus: How what we know about summer learning loss can guide educators, districts, and parents during current school closures.* https://www.gse.harvard.edu/news/20/03/harvard-edcast-learning-loss-and-coronavirus

Anghileri, J. (1995). Language, arithmetic, and the negotiation of meaning. *For the Learning of Mathematics, 15*(3), 10–14.

Atteberry, A., & McEachin, A.. (2016). School's out: Summer learning loss across grade levels and contexts in the United States today. In K. Alexander, S. Pitcock, & M. Boulay (Eds.), *Summer learning and summer learning loss* (pp. 35–54). Teachers College Press.

Baldwin, R., Cintron, S., Coe, P., & Sebelski, S. (2021). *Equitable math instruction: Enacting instruction that is grade-level, engaging, affirming and meaningful.* https://www.unbounded.org/thought-leadership/concept-papers/equitable-math-instruction

Baroody, A. J. (1985). Mastery of basic number combinations: Internalization of relationships or facts? *Journal for Research in Mathematics Education, 16*(2), 83–98. https://doi.org/10.2307/748366

Baroody, A. J. (2006). Why children have difficulties mastering the basic number combinations and how to help them. *Teaching Children Mathematics, 13,* 22–32.

Baumann, T. (2021). *How to engage the emergent bilingual students in your math classroom.* NWEA. Retrieved February 7, 2021, from https://www.nwea.org/blog/2021/how-to-engage-the-emergent-bilingual-students-in-your-math-classroom/

Bay-Williams, J. M., & Kling, G. G. (2019). *Math fact fluency: 60+ games and assessment tools to support learning and retention*. ASCD.

Bay-Williams, J. M., & SanGiovanni, J. J. (2021). *Figuring out fluency in mathematics teaching and learning, Grades K–8: Moving beyond basic facts and memorization*. Corwin.

Beck, I. L., McKeown, M. G., & Kukan, L. (2002). *Bringing words to life: Robust vocabulary instruction*. Guilford Press.

Beck, I. L., McKeown, M. G., & Kukan, L. (2013). *Bringing words to life: Robust vocabulary instruction* (2nd ed.). Guilford Press.

Beck, I. L., McKeown, M. G., & Omanson, R. C. (1987). The effects and uses of diverse vocabulary instructional techniques. In M. G. McKeown & M. E. Curtis (Eds.), *The nature of vocabulary acquisition* (pp. 147–163). Erlbaum.

Bell, L. I. (2005). *12 powerful words that increase test scores and help close the achievement gap. A resource for educations and parents*. https://www.larry-bell.com/product/12-powerful-words/

Benedict, J. (2020). *Students tracking their own data during distance learning*. Visualize Your Learning. Retrieved January 25, 2022, from https://visualizeyourlearning.com/2020/09/06/students-tracking-their-own-data-during-distance-learning/

Blachowicz, C. L. Z., & Fisher, P. J. (2006). *Teaching vocabulary in all classrooms* (3rd ed.). Pearson Education.

Black, P. J., & Wiliam, D. (1998). Assessment and classroom learning. *Assessment in Education: Principles, Policy and Practice, 5*(1), 7–74.

Boaler, J. (2015). *Fluency without fear: Research evidence on the best ways to learn math facts*. Stanford Graduate School of Education. Retrieved February 2, 2022, from https://www.youcubed.org/evidence/fluency-without-fear/

Boonen, A. J. H., van Wesel, F., Jolles, J., & van der Schoot, M. (2014). The role of visual representation type, spatial ability, and reading comprehension in word problem solving: An item-level analysis in elementary school children. *International Journal of Educational Research, 68*(1), 15–26. Retrieved February 25, 2022, from https://www.learntechlib.org/p/203726/

Bravo, M. A., & Cervetti, G. N. (2008). Teaching vocabulary through text and experience in content areas. In A. E. Farstrup & S. J. Samuels (Eds.), *What research has to say about vocabulary instruction* (pp. 130–149). International Reading Association.

Brod, G., Werkle-Bergner, M., & Shing, Y. L. (2013). The influence of prior knowledge on memory: A developmental cognitive neuroscience perspective. *Frontiers in Behavioral Neuroscience, 7*, 139. https://doi.org/10.3389/fnbeh.2013.00139

Brownell, A. (1956/1987). Meaning and skill: Maintaining the balance. *Arithmetic Teacher, 34*(8), 18–25.

Bryant, P. (1997). Mathematical understanding in the nursery school years. In T. Nunes & P. Bryant, (Eds.), *Learning and teaching mathematics: An international perspective* (pp. 53–67). Psychology Press.

Carpenter, T., Fennema, E., Frannke, M., Levi, L., & Empson, S. (1999/2014). *Children's mathematics: Cognitively guided instruction* (2nd ed.). Heinemann.

Cawley, J. F., Parmar, R. S., Foley, T. E., Salmon, S., & Roy, S. (2001). Arithmetic performance of students. Implications for standards and programming. *Exceptional Children, 67*, 311–328.

Colorado Department of Education. (n.d.). *Learning loss recovery strategy guide*. Retrieved January 25, 2022, from https://www.cde.state.co.us/uip/strategyguide-learninglossrecovery

Cooper, H., Nye, B., Charlton, K., Lindsay, J., & Greathouse, S. (1996). The effects of summer vacation on achievement test scores: A narrative and meta-analytic review. *Review of Educational Research, 66*(3), 227–268.

Cramer, K., & Whitney, S. (2010). Learning rational number concepts and skills in elementary classrooms: Translating research to the elementary classroom. In D. V. Lambdin & F. K. Lester (Eds.), *Teaching and learning mathematics: Translating research to the elementary classroom* (pp. 15–22). NCTM.

Crespo, S., Kyriakides, A. O., & McGee, S. (2005). Nothing basic about "basic facts": Exploring addition facts with fourth graders. *Teaching Children Mathematics, 12*(2), 60–67.

Csikszentmihalyi, M. (1997). *Finding flow: The psychology of engagement with everyday life*. Basic Books.

Dale, E. (1965). Vocabulary measurement: Techniques and major findings. *Elementary English, 42*(8), 895–901.

Daro, P., Mosher, F., & Corcoran, T. (2011). *Learning trajectories in mathematics: A Foundation for standards, curriculum, assessment, and instruction*. Philadelphia: Consortium for Policy Research in Education.

David, J. (2008). *What research says about . . . / Grade retention*. Retrieved January 20, 2022, from https://www.ascd.org/el/articles/grade-retention

Davies, A. (2004). *Finding proof of learning in a one-to-one computing classroom*. Connections Publishing.

Davies, A. (2007). Involving students in the classroom assessment process. In D. Reeves (Ed.), *Ahead of the curve: The power to transform teaching and learning* (Kindle ed.). Solution Tree.

Dexter, D. D., & Hughes, C. A. (2011). Graphic organizers and students with learning disabilities: A meta-analysis. *Learning Disability Quarterly, 34*, 51–72.

Dixon, J. (2020). *Just-in-time vs. just-in-case scaffolding: How to foster productive perseverance*. https://www.hmhco.com/blog/just-in-time-vs-just-in-case-scaffolding-how-to-foster-productive-perseverance

Dorn, E., Hancock, B., Sarakatsannis, J., & Viruleg, E. (2021). *Covid-19 and education: The lingering effects of unfinished learning*. Retrieved February 10, 2022, from https://www.mckinsey.com/industries/education/our-insights/covid-19-and-education-the-lingering-effects-of-unfinished-learning

Downton, A. (2008). Links between children's understanding of multiplication and solution strategies for division. In M. Goos, R. Brown, & K. Makar (Eds.), *Navigating currents and charting directions* (pp. 171–178). MERGA.

Ebby, C. B., Hulbert, E. T., & Fletcher, N. (2019). What can we learn from correct answers? *Teaching Children Mathematics, 25*(6), 346–353.

Echevarría, J., & Graves, A. (2007). *Sheltered content instruction: Teaching English language learners with diverse abilities* (3rd ed.). Allyn and Bacon.

Echevarría, J., & Graves, A. (2015). *Sheltered content instruction: Teaching English learners with diverse abilities* (5th ed.). Pearson.

Echevarría, J., Vogt, M. E., & Short, D. (2014). *Making content comprehensible for elementary English language learners: The SIOP model*. Allyn & Bacon.

Ericsson, K. A. (2016). Summing up hours of any type of practice versus identifying optimal practice activities: Commentary on Macnamara, Moreau, & Hambrick (2016). *Perspectives on Psychological Science, 11,* 351–354. https://doi.org/10.1177/1745691616635600

Falchikov, N. (2004). Involving students in assessment. *Psychology Learning and Teaching, 3*(2), 102–108.

Fauzan, A., Yerizon, Y., & Yolanda, R. N. (2020). Learning trajectory for teaching division using RME approach at elementary schools. *Journal of Physis: Conference Series.* https://doi.org/10.1088/1742-6596/1554/1/012079

Feldman, Z. (2012). *Describing pre-service teachers' developing understanding of elementary number theory topics.* Boston University.

Fischbein, E., Deri, M., Nello, M. S., & Marino, M. S. (1985). The role of implicit models in solving verbal problems in multiplication and division. *Journal for Research in Mathematics Education, 16*(1), 3–17. https://doi.org/10.2307/748969

Fong, P. (2021). *High-quality tutoring: An evidence-based strategy to tackle learning loss.* IES: Regional Educational Laboratory Program. Retrieved January 20, 2022, from https://www.wested.org/wested-insights/high-quality-tutoring-an-evidence-based-strategy-to-tackle-learning-loss/

Francisco, A. (2019). *Ask the cognitive scientist: Distributed practice.* Digital Promise. Retrieved February 1, 2022, from https://digitalpromise.org/2019/05/08/ask-the-cognitive-scientist-distributed-practice/#:~:text=Distributed%20practice%20refers%20to%20reviews,event%20(termed%20massed%20practice)

Frey, N. (2005). Retention, social promotion, and academic redshirting: What do we know and need to know? *Remedial and Special Education, 26*(6), 332–346. https://doi.org/10.1177/07419325050260060401

Fuchs, L. S., & Fuchs, D. (1986). Effects of systematic formative evaluation: A meta-analysis. *Exceptional Children, 53*(3), 199–208.

Fuson, K. C. (2003). Toward computational fluency in multidigit multiplication and division. *Teaching Children Mathematics, 9,* 300–305.

Fuson, K. C., & Briars, D. J. (1990). Using a base-ten blocks learning/teaching approach for first- and second-grade place-value and multidigit addition and subtraction. *Journal for Research in Mathematics Education, 21*(3), 180–206. https://doi.org/10.2307/749373

Fuson, K. C., Wearne, D., Hiebert, J. C., Murray, H. G., Human, P. G., Olivier, A. I., Carpenter, T. P., & Fennema, E. (1997). Children's conceptual structures for multidigit numbers and methods of multidigit addition and subtraction. *Journal for Research in Mathematics Education, 28*(2), 130–162. https://doi.org/10.2307/749759

Gersten, R., Chard, D. J., Jayanthi, M., Baker, S. K., Morphy, P., & Flojo, J. (2009). Mathematics instruction for students with learning disabilities: A meta-analysis of instructional components. *Review of Educational Research, 79*(3): 1202–1242. https://doi 10.3102/0034654309334431

Ginsburg, H. P. (1987). The development of arithmetic thinking. In D. D. Hammill (Ed.), *Assessing the abilities and instructional needs of students* (pp. 423–440). PRO-ED.

Glazebrook, K. (2015). "The effectiveness of graphic organizers on students' attitudes towards, approaches to, and accuracy when solving word problems." *Student Research Submissions, 181.* https://scholar.umw.edu/student_research/181

Gonzalez, N., Moll, L. C., & Amanti, C. (Eds.). (2005). *Funds of knowledge.* Routledge.

Götze, D. (2018). Fostering a conceptual understanding of division: A language-and mathematics-integrated project in primary school. In N. Planas & M. Schütte (Eds.), *Proceedings of the Fourth ERME Topic Conference 'Classroom-based research on mathematics and language'* (pp. 73–80). Technical University of Dresden/ERME.

Guskey, T. R. (2007). Using assessments to improve teaching and learning. In D. Reeves (Ed.), *Ahead of the curve: The power of assessment to transform teaching and learning* (Kindle ed.). Solution Tree.

Guskey, T. R., & Pigott, T. D. (1988). Research on group-based mastery learning programs: A meta-analysis. *The Journal of Educational Research, 81*(4), 197–216. https://doi.org/10.1080/00220671.1988.10885824

Hammond, J., & Gibbons, P. (2005). Putting scaffolding to work: The contribution of scaffolding in articulating ESL education. *Prospect, 20*(1), 6–30.

Hancock, A. (2021). *Why unfinished instruction is more accurate and equitable than learning loss.* Retrieved February 20, 2022, from https://www.unbounded.org/blog/why-unfinished-instruction-is-more-accurate-and-equitable-than-learning-loss

Harper, C., & de Jong, E. (2004). Misconceptions about teaching English language learners. *Journal of Adolescent & Adult Literacy, 48,* 152–162.

Hattie, J. A. (1992). Measuring the effects of schooling. *Australian Journal of Education, 36*(1), 5–13.

Hattie, J. A. (2018). *Hattie ranking: 252 influences and effect sizes related to student achievement.* Retrieved January 26, 2022, from https://visible-learning.org/hattie-ranking-influences-effect-sizes-learning-achievement/

Henry, V., & Brown, R. (2008). First-grade basics: An investigation into teaching and learning of an accelerated, high-demand memorization standard. *Journal for Research in Mathematics Education, 39*(2), 153–183.

Hiebert, E. H. (2019). *Teaching words and how they work: Small changes for big vocabulary results.* Teachers College Press.

Hiebert, E. H., & Kamil, M. L. (2005). *Teaching and learning vocabulary: Bringing research to practice.* Erlbaum.

Institute of Education Sciences (IES). (2009). *Assisting students struggling with mathematics: Response to intervention (RtI) for elementary and middle schools.* Retrieved February 3, 2022, from https://ies.ed.gov/ncee/wwc/practiceguide/2

IRIS Center. (2022). *Progress monitoring.* Retrieved January 30, 2022, from https://iris.peabody.vanderbilt.edu/module/dbi2/cresource/q2/p03/

Jackson, J., & Narvaez, R. (2013, September). Interactive word walls: Create a tool to increase science vocabulary in five easy steps. *Science and Children, 51*(1), 42–49. https://doi.org/10.2505/4/sc13_051_01_42

James, G. (2019). *What goal-setting does to your brain and why it's spectacularly effective: Goal setting is a scientifically proven way to restructure your brain cells so that you're massively more successful.* Retrieved February 5, 2022, from https://www.inc.com/geoffrey-james/what-goal-setting-does-to-your-brain-why-its-spectacularly-effective.html

Jenkins, J. R., Stein, M. L., & Wysocki, K. (1984). Learning vocabulary through reading. *American Educational Research Journal, 21*(4), 767–787. https://doi.org/10.2307/1163000

Kamin, S. J., & Lamb, A. J. (2021). *Grade retention after Covid-19: Evidence-based guidance.* Retrieved January 30, 2022, from https://education.uconn.edu/2021/10/20/grade-retention-after-covid-19-evidence-based-guidance/

Kelly, J., Lesaux, N., Kieffer, M., & Faller, S. (2010). Effective academic vocabulary instruction in the urban middle school. *The Reading Teacher, 64*(1), 5–14. https://doi.org/10.1598/RT.64.1.1or http://www.cal.org/create/conferences/2012/pdfs/effective-academic%20-vocabulary-instruction-in-the-urban-middle-school.pdf

Koutstaal, W., Buckner, R. L., Schacter, D., & Rosen, B. R. (1997, March 23–25). *Presentation at of the Fourth Annual Meeting of the Cognitive Neuroscience Society*, Boston, p. 68.

Krawec, J., Huang, J., Montague, M., Kressler, B., & Meliá de Alba, A. (2013). The effects of cognitive strategy instruction on knowledge of math problem-solving processes of middle school students with learning disabilities. *Learning Disability Quarterly, 36*(2), 80–92. https://doi.org/10.1177/0731948712463368

Lager, C. (2006). Types of mathematics–language reading interactions that unnecessarily hinder algebra learning and assessment. *Reading Psychology, 27,* 165–204.

Lajoie, C., & Maheux, J. (2013). Richness and complexity of teaching division: Prospective elementary teachers' roleplaying on a division with remainder. *Proceedings of the Eighth Congress of European Research in Mathematics Education (CERME 8).* Manavgat-Side, Turkey.

Lehtinen, E., Hannula-Sormunen, M., McMullen, J., & Gruber, H. (2017). Cultivating mathematical skills: From drill-and-practice to deliberate practice. *ZDM Mathematics Education, 49*(4), 625–636.

Levine, S., & Pantoja, N. (2021). Development of children's math attitudes: Gender differences, key socializers, and intervention approaches. *Developmental Review, 62,* 100997. https://doi.org/10.1016/j.dr.2021.100997

Li, D. (2017). *Why student data should be students' data.* Retrieved January 25, 2022, from https://www.edutopia.org/article/why-student-data-should-be-students-data

Loft. (2019). *Prior knowledge: Connect to what students know.* Retrieved January 25, 2022, from https://guides.loft.io/learning/conceive/principles/prior-knowledge/

Lundgren, C. (n.d.). *Tapping into prior knowledge.* Colorín Colorado. Retrieved January 20, 2022, from https://www.colorincolorado.org/video/tapping-prior-knowledge

Ma, L. (1999). *Knowing and teaching elementary mathematics: Teachers' understanding of fundamental mathematics in China and the United States.* Erlbaum.

Mancilla-Martinez, J. (2010). Word meanings matter: Cultivating English vocabulary knowledge in fifth-grade Spanish speaking language minority learners. *TESOL Quarterly, 44*(4), 669–699.

Marzano, R. J. (2004). *Building background knowledge for academic achievement: Research on what works in schools.* ASCD.

Marzano, R. J. (2006). *Classroom assessment and grading that work.* ASCD.

Marzano, R. J. (2007). Designing a comprehensive approach to classroom assessment. In D. Reeves (Ed.), *Ahead of the curve: The power to transform teaching and learning* (Kindle ed., pp. 103–125). Solution Tree.

Merkley, D. M., & Jefferies, D. (2001). Guidelines for implementing a graphic organizer. The Reading Teacher, 54(4), 350–357.

Merriam-Webster. Remediation. In *Merriam-Webster.com dictionary.* Retrieved February 1, 2022, from https://www.merriam-webster.com/dictionary/

Milner, H. R., IV. (2012). Beyond a test score: Explaining opportunity gaps in education practice. *Journal of Black Studies, 43*(6), 693–718.

Ministry of Education, New Zealand. (2009). Self-efficacy in mathematics. In *Student learning approaches for tomorrow's world. Results of New Zealand 15-year-olds in the 2003 PISA survey* (pp. 18–19). Retrieved January 30, 2022, from https://www

.educationcounts.govt.nz/publications/schooling/pisa-2003-student-learning
-approaches-for-tomorrows-world/self-efficacy-in-mathematics#:~:text=
Self%2Defficacy%20in%20mathematics%20indicates,obstacles%20to%20
solving%20maths%20problems.&text=As%20an%20indicator%20of%20
self,at%20various%20specific%20mathematics%20tasks

Mitchell, M. (2021, June 24). *Acceleration vs. remediation vs. intervention: What's the difference?* Edmentum. https://blog.edmentum.com/acceleration-vs-remediation-vs-intervention-whats-difference

Nagy, W., & Townsend, D. (2012). Words as tools: Learning academic vocabulary as language acquisition. *Reading Research Quarterly, 47*(1), 91–108. https://doi.org/10.1002/RRQ.011

Nakamura, J., & Csikszentmihalyi, M. (2009). Flow theory and research. In S. J. Lopez & C. R. Snyder (Eds.), *Oxford handbook of positive psychology* (pp. 195–206). Oxford University Press.

Nash, H., & Snowling, M. (2006). Teaching new words to children with poor existing vocabulary knowledge: A controlled evaluation of the definition and context methods. *International Journal of Language & Communication Disorders, 41*(3), 335–354. https://doi.org/10.1080/13682820600602295

National Center on Intensive Intervention. (n.d.). *Mathematics progress monitoring. Intensive intervention in mathematics course: Module 2 overview.* Retrieved January 30, 2022, from https://intensiveintervention.org/progress-monitoring-math-course

National Council of Teachers of Mathematics (NCTM). (2000). *Principles and standards for school mathematics.*

National Governors Association Center for Best Practices & Council of Chief State School Officers (NGA & CCSSO). (2010). *Common Core State Standards for Mathematics.*

National Research Council (NRC). (2001). *Adding it up: Helping children learn mathematics.* J. Kilpatrick, J. Swafford, & B. Findell (Eds.). National Academy Press. https://doi.org/10.17226/9822

Neagoy, M. (2008). *Unpacking fractions.* ASCD.

Nisbet, J. (2021). *Should we be focusing on learning loss or unfinished learning?* Retrieved December 26, 2022, from https://www.prodigygame.com/main-en/blog/learning-loss-unfinished-learning/#:~:text=Unfinished%20learning%20is%20an%20educational,had%20the%20opportunity%20to%20learn

Ogle, D. (1986). K-W-L: A teaching model that develops active reading of expository text. *The Reading Teacher, 39,* 564–570.

Pajares, F., & Graham, L. (1999). Self-efficacy, motivation constructs, and mathematics performance of entering middle school students. *Contemporary Educational Psychology, 24*(2), 124–139.

Rathmell, E. C. (1978). Using thinking strategies to learn the basic facts. In M. Suydan (Ed.), *1978 Yearbook of the National Council of Teachers of Mathematics.*

Roberts, T. (2018). *Two essential (learning) design questions.* Retrieved January 25, 2022, from http://www.tracyroberts.ca/?p=1603

Robinson, K. M., Arbuthnott, K. D., Rose, D., McCarron, M. C., Globa, C. A., & Phonexay, S. D. (2006). Stability and change in children's division strategies. *Journal of Experimental Child Psychology, 93,* 224–238.

Robinson, K. M., & LeFevre, J. A. (2012). The inverse relation between multiplication and division: Concepts, procedures, and a cognitive framework. *Educational Studies in Mathematics, 79,* 409–428.

look up ✗

Rollins, S. P. (2014). *Learning in the fast lane: 8 ways to put all students on the road to academic success.* (Kindle ed.). ASCD.

Rosenshine, B. (1987). Explicit teaching and teacher training. *Journal of Teacher Education, 38*(3), 34–36.

Ryan, E. (2019). *Three ways to better engage students to get the most from educational assessments.* NWEA. Retrieved January 30, 2022, from https://www.nwea.org/blog/2019three-ways-to-better-engage-students-to-get-the-most-from-educational-assessments/

Safer, N., & Fleischman, S. (2005). How student progress monitoring improves instruction. *Educational Leadership, 62*(5), 81–83.

Schmoker, M. (1999). *The key to continuous school improvement.* ASCD.

Scott, J., Jamieson-Noel, D., & Asselin, M. (2003). Vocabulary instruction throughout the day in twenty-three Canadian upper-elementary classrooms. *The Elementary School Journal, 103*(3), 269–286.

Shulman, L. S. (1986). Those who understand: Knowledge growth in teaching. *Educational Researcher, 15*(2), 4–14.

Silva, J. (2019). The math agency of three emergent bilinguals with identified learning disabilities. Proceedings of the 41st Annual Meeting of the North American Chapter of the International Group for the Psychology of Mathematics Education. Retrieved February 10, 2022, from https://www.researchgate.net/publication/338852445_the_math_agency_of_three_emergent_bilinguals_with_identified_learning_disabilities

Silver, E., & Kitchen, R. (Eds.). (2010). *Linguistic complexity in mathematics assessments: Vol. 2. Assessing English language learners in mathematics.* Research Monograph 2. TODOS: Mathematics for All.

Smith, A., Angotti, R., & Fink, L. (2012). Why are there so many words in math? Planning for content-area vocabulary instruction. *Voices from the Middle, 20*(1), 43.

Sousa, D., & Tomlinson, C. (2011). *Differentiation and the brain: How neuroscience supports the learner-friendly classroom.* Solution Tree.

Stahl, A., & Stahl, K. (2004). Word wizards all! Teaching word meanings in preschool and primary education. In J. F. Baumann & E. J. Kame'enui (Eds.), *Vocabulary instruction: Research to practice* (pp. 59–78). Guilford Press.

Stahl, K. (2008). The effects of three instructional methods on the reading comprehension and content acquisition of novice readers. *Journal of Literacy Research, 40*(3), 359–393. https://doi.org/10.1080/10862960802520594

Stein, M., & Bovalino, J. (2001). Reflections on practice. Manipulatives: One piece of the puzzle. *Mathematics Teaching in the Middle School, 6*(6), 356–359. http://www.jstor.org/stable/41180973

Steinberg, R. M. (1985). Instruction on derived facts strategies in addition and subtraction. *Journal for Research in Mathematics Education, 16*(5), 337–355. https://doi.org/10.2307/749356

Stiggins, R. (2007). Assessment for learning: An essential foundation of productive instruction. In D. Reeves (Ed.), *Ahead of the curve: The power to transform teaching and learning* (Kindle ed., pp. 59–77). Solution Tree.

Strangman, N., Vue, G., Hall, T., & Meyer A. (2004 [links updated 2014]). Graphic organizers and implications for universal design for learning: Curriculum enhancement report. National Center on Accessing the General Curriculum. http:

//www.cast.org/binaries/content/assets/common/publications/aem/ncac-graphic-organizers-udl-2014-10.docx

Tankersley, K. (2005). *Literacy strategies for Grades 4–12: Reinforcing the threads of reading.* ASCD.

Thomas B. Fordham Institute. (2021). *Addressing unfinished learning with targeted help and high-dosage tutoring.* Retrieved on December 26, 2021, from https://fordham institute.org/national/commentary/addressing-unfinished-learning-targeted-help-and-high-dosage-tutoring

U.S. Department of Education. (2021). *ED COVID handbook: Vol. 2. Roadmap to reopening safely and meeting all students' needs.* OPEPD-IO-21-02. https://www2.ed.gov/documents/coronavirus/reopening-2.pdf

Webb, N. (2002). *An analysis of the alignment between mathematics standards and assessments for three states* [Paper presentation]. Annual Meeting of the American Educational Research Association, New Orleans, LA. https:// www.researchgate.ne/publication/252605969_An_Analysis_of_the_Alignment_Between_Mathematics_Standards_and_Assessments_for_Three_States

Wesche, M., & Paribakht, T. S. (1996). Assessing second language vocabulary knowledge: Depth versus breadth. *Canadian Modern Language Review, 53*(1), 13–40.

Willis, J. (2006). Research-based strategies to ignite student learning: Insights from a neurologist and classroom teacher (Kindle ed.). ASCD.

Wright, W. (2015). *Foundations for teaching English language learners: Research, theory, policy and practice.* Caslon.

World Bank. (2021). *Learning losses from Covid-19 could cost this generation of students close to $17 trillion in lifetime earning.* Retrieved February 24, 2022, from https://www.worldbank.org/en/news/press-release/2021/12/06/learning-losses-from-covid-19-could-cost-this-generation-of-students-close-to-17-trillion-in-lifetime-earnings#:~:text=WASHINGTON%2C%20DC%2C%20Dec.,Bank%2C%20UNESCO%2C%20and%20UNICEF

Zhang, D., Ding, Y., Stegall, J., & Mo, L. (2012). The effect of visual-chunking-representation accommodation on geometry testing for students with math disabilities. *Learning Disabilities Research & Practice, 27,* 167–177.

Zollman, A. (2009). Mathematical graphic organizers. *Teaching Children Mathematics, 16*(4), 222–229.

Zwiers, J. (2008). *Building academic language: Essential practices for content classrooms, Grades 5–12.* Jossey-Bass.

About Dr. Nicki

Dr. Nicki Newton is an education consultant who works with schools and districts around the United States and Canada on K–8 math curriculum. She has taught elementary school, middle school, and graduate school. Dr Nicki has an Ed.M. and an Ed.D. from the Department of Curriculum and Teaching at Teachers College, Columbia University, specializing in Teacher Education and Curriculum Development. She is greatly interested in teaching and learning practices around the world and has researched education in Denmark, Guatemala, and India. She has written more than 30 books and is an avid pinner, blogger, and tweeter. Dr. Nicki will Zoom into any book study group to chat: Email her at drnicki7@gmail.com